QUICK & EASY BAKING

Duncan Hines

WITH CAKE MIXES

PUBLICATIONS INTERNATIONAL, LTD.

Contents

Copyright © 1986 by Procter & Gamble

CARVAJAL S.A.
Impreso en Colombia
Printed in Colombia

Library of Congress Catalog Card Number: 85-062862
ISBN: 0-88176-821-9

Cover design: Inez Smith
Photography: Cy DeCosse Creative, Minneapolis
Recipe Development: Culinary Arts & Services, Chicago

On the front cover: Luscious Chocolate Party Cake
On the back cover: Calypso Cake, Carrot Muffins, Golden Fruit Loaves, and Wheat Germ Cookies

Success Tips For Cakes

BAKING CAKES

Prepare the Baking Pans

Be sure to use the correct pan size for each recipe, which usually is stamped on the bottom of the pan. An incorrect pan size affects the baking time and may cause your baked product to rise improperly, shrink, or overflow the pan.

Shiny metal pans are preferred for even baking. Oven-proof glass pans may be used also, but reduce the oven temperature by 25°F.

Follow recipe instructions for preparing pans. When an ungreased pan is specified, the use of a greased pan may ruin your cake.

When a recipe calls for greased and floured pans, do this step before mixing the batter. It is important to bake the batter immediately after mixing. Grease each pan generously using at least ½ tablespoon of shortening for each pan. Apply the shortening evenly with a brush or wax paper. Sprinkle flour in pan and tilt to distribute the flour evenly.

Mix the Batter

Mixing batter is the easiest part of baking a cake. An electric mixer will do most of the work for you. Usually, the first step is simply to blend all the ingredients just until they are moistened; use the mixer on low speed or combine the ingredients by hand with a wooden spoon.

The second step is to beat the ingredients, scraping down the sides of the bowl often with a rubber spatula, until enough air has been incorporated to make the cake rise high and fluffy. Use the speed recommended on your portable or standard mixer.

Follow the beating time indicated in the recipe or on the cake mix package, making sure you do not underbeat or overbeat. (Underbeating does not incorporate enough air; overbeating releases the air previously incorporated and undoes your work.) Set your kitchen timer for perfect accuracy.

Always bake cakes immediately after mixing the batter.

Bake

First, remember to preheat your oven to the temperature specified in the recipe or on the cake mix package for a full 15 to 20 minutes.

Baking at the proper oven temperature is extremely important, since overbaking or underbaking is the most common cause of less-than-perfect cakes. If you doubt the reliability of your oven thermostat, check it with an oven thermometer. Simply set the oven and place the thermometer inside for 20 to 30 minutes. If they do not agree, the oven setting must be adjusted accordingly.

Even heating is important, too. If two oven racks are used, stagger the pans to avoid having one pan directly over another. If a single rack is used, position it so that the pans are as near the center of the oven as possible. Do not allow pans to touch each other or sides of oven. Do not open the oven door until you think cake is done; heat is lost quickly.

A kitchen timer, if your oven thermostat is accurate, will tell you approximately when the cake should be done. Before the cake is removed from the oven, however, it must be tested for doneness.

To test cakes insert a toothpick in the center. When done, the toothpick will come out perfectly clean.

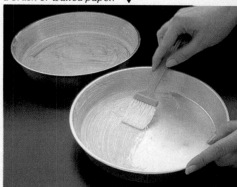

To grease pans, apply shortening evenly with a brush or waxed paper. ▼

To flour pans, sprinkle in flour and tilt to distribute flour evenly. ▼

If baking on one oven rack, two pans should not touch each other or sides of oven. ▼

Cake is done if toothpick inserted in the center comes out perfectly clean. ▼

Test beaten egg whites by cutting through to bottom of mixture with a spatula. ▼

For best results, apply frosting with a small metal spatula. ▼

To split evenly, insert toothpicks around center of layer; cut with a serrated knife. ▼

Sift confectioners' sugar over doily placed on top of unfrosted cake; then lift doily. ▼

Cooling Cakes

Cool layer cakes in pans on wire racks for at least 10 minutes, but not more than 20 minutes. Then gently loosen sides of cake with a spatula.

To remove a layer cake from the pan, wrap a dish towel around a wire rack (so it won't leave an imprint), place it on top of the pan, and invert the pan and rack together. Remove the pan and your cake will be upside down on the protected rack.

Then, to get the cake right-side-up, place another rack on the bottom of the cake and turn over both racks with the cake between them. When the protected rack is removed, your cake will be right-side-up on a wire rack, where it should stay to finish cooling. Always use wire racks so that air can circulate evenly around the cake.

For a cake that is rolled, like a jelly-roll cake, turn out the cake and roll it in a towel while still warm enough to be shaped. When cool, it can be unrolled, spread with a filling, and rerolled without the towel.

TIPS FOR ANGEL FOOD CAKES

Follow the package directions carefully. Much thorough testing has gone into developing them.

Be sure the bowl, beaters, and spatula are really clean! Even the smallest trace of grease on them will keep egg whites from whipping properly.

For the best cake, beat the egg whites until they hold a very stiff peak. Test the egg whites by cutting through to the bottom of the mixture with a spatula—egg whites should hold the trench shape and not run together at the bottom of the bowl.

Bake on the lowest oven rack position but not on the floor of the oven. If there are two racks, remove the top one. Duncan Hines Angel Food Cakes rise high and need plenty of room. To cool, hang the pan upside down on a funnel or bottle at least 1½ hours. To remove cake from pan, loosen edges with knife.

FROSTING CAKES

Before frosting any cake, let it cool completely. Never frost a warm cake unless the recipe directs you to do so. Brush off any loose crumbs, which tend to mix in with the frosting. If necessary, a thin coating of frosting, applied first, will seal in any remaining crumbs. For the best-looking cakes, swirl the frosting in a decorative way as it is applied. The best tool for frosting is a small metal spatula.

To catch any drips and keep the cake plate neat, place four pieces of wax paper under edges of the bottom layer, which will slide out after the cake is frosted.

To frost a 2-layer cake, place one layer upside-down on a plate, and spread about one-fourth of the frosting on top. Then place the second layer right-side up on top of the frosted layer. Frost the sides first with about two-thirds of the remaining frosting; then frost the top.

Some recipes require the cutting of layers into two thin layers before applying the frosting. To split a layer evenly, measure its height with a ruler and mark off the center point with toothpicks inserted around the cake. Then cut across the tops of the toothpicks with a long serrated knife, using a sawing motion.

DECORATING CAKES

Here are some simple cake decorating ideas that will dress up your cakes quickly and easily.

Decorate an unfrosted cake by placing a paper doily on top and sifting confectioners' sugar heavily over the doily. Lift the doily carefully and you will have an imprint of its design on the cake.

Use the tip of a knife to score the top of a chocolate or white frosted cake into six or eight triangles. Fill alternate triangles with chopped walnuts, peanuts, cashews, or pistachio nuts.

Tint shredded coconut with one or two drops of food coloring dissolved in a teaspoon of water. Shake in a jar. Create several colors of shredded coconut and sprinkle them like confetti, over the cake.

Melt semisweet chocolate, spread in circle between pieces of wax paper, and let harden in the refrigerator. Then remove one sheet of wax paper, cut the chocolate into wedges, and lift them off with a small spatula. Decorate the top of your cake with the wedges.

Using a teaspoon, drizzle melted chocolate in parallel lines across a white frosted sheet cake. Then draw a knife down through the lines to create a feathered, criss-cross effect.

To decorate truly fancy cakes, you will need a pastry bag fitted with various decorator tips. With a little practice, you will be able to make lovely designs. Be careful not to fill the bag more than half full and to apply even pressure. (A toss-away decorator bag can be improvised by rolling and taping a 15-inch triangle of parchment paper and snipping off the tip.)

AT HIGH ALTITUDE

If you live in an area above 3500 feet, you must adjust the recipes according to the specific instructions on each Duncan Hines Cake Mix package.

High altitude baked goods have a tendency to stick to the pan. Be sure to grease the pans generously before dusting with flour. Fill the pans only half full with batter; otherwise, high altitude cakes may overflow the pan. Use eggs that are cold, not at room temperature.

For answers to other high altitude baking problems, contact the home economics department of your state college, the state agricultural extension service, or the home service department of your local utility company,

STORING CAKES

Cakes, except fruitcakes, are at their best the day they are made. But, if stored properly, most cakes will remain fresh for several days.

Unfrosted cakes must be cooled completely before being wrapped and stored, or they will become soggy. Cakes with creamy frostings may be stored in a cake keeper, under an inverted bowl, or loosely covered with aluminum foil or plastic wrap.

Cakes with cooked-type frostings do not store well. But leftovers may be stored in a cake keeper or under an inverted bowl, provided a knife or spatula is inserted under the edge to keep it from being airtight.

Whipped cream cakes (either topped or filled), cheesecakes, or cakes containing cream cheese, sour cream, or yogurt must be refrigerated.

FREEZING & THAWING

Unfrosted cakes freeze well for up to 4 months. Place them on cardboard and wrap them in aluminum foil or plastic wrap. Thaw at room temperature, wrapped or unwrapped.

Frosted cakes can be frozen about 2 months, wrapped in aluminum foil or plastic wrap. To prevent the frosting from sticking to the wrapping, freeze the cake before wrapping it. Or insert toothpicks in the sides and top of the cake to hold the wrapping away, making sure not to puncture the wrapping. Thaw at room temperature.

Whipped cream cakes should be treated like frosted cakes, and may be frozen for the same length of time. Thaw in the refrigerator for several hours. Or thaw individual servings on plates for 5 minutes.

Cakes with fruit or custard fillings are not recommended for freezing; they become soggy when thawed.

Place flat wedges of semisweet chocolate on top of cake for attractive decoration. ▼

Draw knife through lines of drizzled melted chocolate to create criss-cross effect. ▼

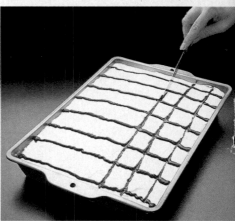

When storing cake with cooked-type frosting, insert knife under edge of cake keeper. ▼

Before freezing, insert toothpicks in cake to keep frosting from sticking to wrapping. ▼

Easy Cakes for Everyday

BANANA SPLIT CAKES

1 package Duncan Hines
   Deluxe Chocolate Chip
   Cake Mix
3 large eggs
⅓ cup Crisco Oil or Puritan
   Oil
1 cup water
3 medium bananas
   Lemon juice
4 cups whipped topping
1 jar (12 ounces) chocolate
   fudge topping
⅓ cup chopped nuts
15 red maraschino cherries

1. Preheat oven to 350°F. Grease and flour 13×9×2-inch pan.

2. Combine dry cake mix, eggs, oil and water in large mixer bowl. Mix, bake and cool cake as directed on package.

3. To serve, peel and slice bananas. Sprinkle with lemon juice to prevent darkening; set aside.

4. Spread 2 cups of whipped topping over cooled cake. Cut cake into 15 pieces (about 3×2½ inches). Top each piece with several banana slices, a dollop of whipped topping and about 1 tablespoon fudge topping. Sprinkle with chopped nuts and top with maraschino cherry. Refrigerate any leftover cake.

BUTTERSCOTCH SWIRL RING CAKE

1 package (4-serving-size)
   butterscotch instant
   pudding and pie filling mix
1 package Duncan Hines
   Deluxe White Cake Mix
2 large eggs
1⅓ cups water
7 tablespoons butter or
   margarine, softened
½ cup packed dark brown
   sugar
2 tablespoons all-purpose
   flour
1 tablespoon light corn syrup
2 tablespoons milk
1 cup confectioners' sugar

1. Preheat oven to 350°F. Heavily grease and flour 10-inch fluted tube pan. Reserve 3 tablespoons pudding mix for glaze.

2. Combine dry cake mix, remaining pudding mix, eggs, water and 4 tablespoons butter in large mixer bowl. Mix batter as directed on package.

3. Reserve 1 cup batter; spread remaining batter in pan. Mix together reserved 1 cup batter, brown sugar and flour. Spoon in ring on batter. Using spoon, fold brown sugar mixture into batter; go around pan twice and avoid scraping sides of pan.

4. Bake at 350°F for 40 to 50 minutes or until toothpick inserted in center comes out clean. Cool in pan on rack 25 minutes. Remove from pan and place on serving plate.

4. For glaze, combine 3 tablespoons butter, reserved 3 tablespoons pudding mix, corn syrup and milk in small saucepan. Heat and stir until butter melts. Remove from heat; add confectioners' sugar, beating until frosting is of desired consistency. Drizzle glaze over warm cake.

Banana Split Cakes

Dump Cake

DUMP CAKE

12 to 16 servings

1   can (20 ounces) crushed
    pineapple in syrup,
    undrained
1   can (21 ounces) cherry pie
    filling
1   package Duncan Hines
    Deluxe Yellow Cake Mix
1   cup chopped pecans
½   cup (1 stick) butter or
    margarine, cut in thin slices

1. Preheat oven to 350°F. Grease 13×9×2-inch pan.

2. Spoon undrained pineapple into pan; spread evenly. Add pie filling and spread in even layer. Sprinkle dry cake mix onto cherry layer; spread evenly. Sprinkle pecans over cake mix. Place butter over top.

3. Bake at 350°F for 48 to 53 minutes. Serve warm or cooled.

PINEAPPLE UPSIDE-DOWN CAKE

12 to 16 servings

1   cup butter or margarine,
    divided
1   cup packed brown sugar
1   can (20 ounces) pineapple
    slices, drained
    Red maraschino cherry
    halves, drained
1   package Duncan Hines
    Butter Recipe Golden
    Cake Mix
3   large eggs
⅔   cup water

1. Preheat oven to 375°F.

2. Melt ½ cup butter in 13×9×2-inch pan. Sprinkle brown sugar evenly in pan. Arrange pineapple slices on sugar. Place cherry halves rounded side down in center of each slice.

3. Combine dry cake mix, eggs, ½ cup soft butter and water in large mixer bowl. Mix cake as directed on package. Pour batter over fruit and spread evenly.

4. Bake at 375°F for 45 to 55 minutes or until toothpick inserted in center comes out clean. Let stand 5 minutes to set topping. Loosen cake from pan and invert onto serving platter.

LEMON TAKE-ALONG CAKE

16 servings

1 package Duncan Hines Deluxe White Cake Mix
1 package (3 ounces) lemon-flavored gelatin
¾ cup water
4 large eggs
¾ cup Crisco Oil or Puritan Oil
1 cup confectioners' sugar
¼ teaspoon grated lemon peel
¼ cup fresh lemon juice

1. Preheat oven to 350°F. Grease 13×9×2-inch pan.

2. Combine dry cake mix, gelatin, water, eggs and oil in large mixer bowl. Beat 5 minutes at medium speed. Turn into pan and spread evenly.

3. Bake at 350°F for 35 to 40 minutes or until toothpick inserted in center comes out clean. Cool in pan on rack 20 to 25 minutes.

4. Poke holes through top of cake with toothpick, spacing holes about 1 inch apart.

5. For glaze, combine confectioners' sugar, lemon peel and lemon juice. Pour over warm cake.

MOCHA CHARMER

16 servings

1 package Duncan Hines Deluxe Swiss Chocolate Cake Mix
4 tablespoons powdered instant coffee
4 large eggs
½ cup Crisco Oil or Puritan Oil
1⅓ cups water
Blanched almonds
½ ounce (½ square) semisweet chocolate, melted
¼ cup Crisco shortening
¼ cup unsweetened cocoa
⅛ teaspoon salt
2¼ cups confectioners' sugar
2 tablespoons milk
½ teaspoon vanilla extract

1. Preheat oven to 350°F. Grease and flour 13×9×2-inch pan.

2. Place dry cake mix, 3 tablespoons instant coffee, 3 eggs, oil and water in large mixer bowl. Mix, bake and cool cake as directed on package.

3. Dip top of each almond in melted chocolate. Place on wax paper and refrigerate until chocolate sets.

4. For frosting*, combine shortening, 1 egg, cocoa, 1 tablespoon instant coffee and salt in bowl. Add confectioners' sugar alternately with milk, beating until smooth. Blend in vanilla. Add more confectioners' sugar to thicken or milk to thin frosting as needed. Spread on cooled cake and decorate with chocolate-tipped almonds.

Or in medium bowl, dissolve 1 teaspoon instant coffee powder in 1 teaspoon hot water; stir in 1 can Duncan Hines Chocolate Frosting.

Mocha Charmer

SWEET CHOCOLATE MOUSSE CAKE

16 servings

1 package Duncan Hines
  Butter Recipe
  Fudge Cake Mix
3 large eggs
½ cup (1 stick) butter or
  margarine, softened
¾ cup water
2 packages (4 ounces each)
  sweet baking chocolate
¼ cup water
6 large eggs, separated
1 teaspoon vanilla extract

1. Preheat oven to 375°F. Grease and flour two 8×1½-inch round layer pans.

2. Combine dry cake mix, 3 eggs, butter and ¾ cup water in large mixer bowl. Mix, bake and cool cake as directed on package.

3. Combine chocolate and ¼ cup water in top of double boiler. Heat over simmering, not boiling, water until melted. Cool slightly.

4. Beat 6 egg whites in large bowl until stiff, not dry, peaks form.

5. Beat 6 egg yolks in large bowl until thick (about 3 minutes); beat in chocolate mixture and vanilla extract. Fold in beaten egg whites. Refrigerate 30 minutes.

6. Cut each cooled layer into 8 wedges and arrange in 9-inch round layer pan so wedges are separated. Pour half of mousse over cake in each pan. Gently spread to fill spaces between wedges. Refrigerate until set.

LEMON PEAR UPSIDE-DOWN CAKE

12 to 16 servings

½ cup (1 stick) butter or
  margarine
1 cup packed brown sugar
1 can (29 ounces) pear
  halves in syrup
  Red maraschino cherry
  halves
1 package Duncan Hines
  Deluxe Lemon Cake Mix
3 large eggs
⅓ cup Crisco Oil or Puritan
  Oil
  Sweetened whipped
  cream

1. Preheat oven to 350°F.

2. Melt butter in 13×9×2-inch pan. Sprinkle brown sugar evenly in pan. Drain pears; reserve syrup. Cut pear halves in quarters. Arrange pears and cherries in pan.

3. Add enough water to reserved pear syrup to make 1¼ cups. Place dry cake mix, liquid, eggs and oil in large mixer bowl. Mix cake as directed on package. Turn into pan and spread evenly over fruit.

4. Bake at 350°F for 45 to 50 minutes or until toothpick inserted in center comes out clean. Let stand for 5 minutes. Invert on large platter. Serve with whipped cream.

SOUR CREAM CHOCOLATE POUND CAKE

12 to 16 servings

1 package Duncan Hines
  Deluxe Sour Cream
  Chocolate Cake Mix
4 large eggs
½ cup Crisco Oil or
  Puritan Oil
1¼ cups water
1 package (4-serving-size)
  chocolate instant pudding
  and pie filling mix
2 tablespoons unsweetened
  cocoa
1 tablespoon plus 2
  teaspoons water
1 tablespoon Crisco Oil or
  Puritan Oil
1 tablespoon corn syrup
1 cup confectioners' sugar

1. Preheat oven to 350°F. Grease and flour 10-inch tube pan.

2. Combine dry cake mix, eggs, ½ cup oil, 1¼ cups water and pudding mix in large mixer bowl. Mix cake as directed on package. Turn batter into pan and spread evenly.

3. Bake at 350°F for 50 to 60 minutes or until toothpick inserted in center comes out clean. Cool in pan on rack 25 minutes. Remove from pan; cool completely on rack.

4. For cocoa glaze, combine cocoa, 1 tablespoon plus 2 teaspoons water, 1 tablespoon oil and corn syrup in small saucepan. Cook and stir over low heat until mixture is smooth. Remove from heat; immediately beat in confectioners' sugar. Drizzle over cake.

GOLDEN CRUNCH CAKE

20 servings

2 cups fine vanilla wafer crumbs
1 cup finely chopped pecans
½ cup sugar
¼ cup (½ stick) butter or margarine
1 package Duncan Hines Butter Recipe Golden Cake Mix
3 large eggs
½ cup (1 stick) butter or margarine, softened
⅔ cup water

1. Preheat oven to 375°F. Grease two 9×5×3-inch pans.

2. Combine wafer crumbs, pecans and sugar in bowl. Add ¼ cup butter and cut in with pastry blender until crumbs are fine. Divide evenly in pans; press on bottom and sides.

3. Combine dry cake mix, eggs, ½ cup butter and water in large mixer bowl. Mix cake as directed on package. Divide batter evenly in pans.

4. Bake at 375°F for 50 to 60 minutes or until toothpick inserted in center comes out clean. Cool in pans on racks 5 minutes. Carefully loosen cake from pans and turn upside down on racks; cool completely.

RAISIN-FILLED ORANGE CAKE

12 to 16 servings

1 package Duncan Hines Deluxe Orange Cake Mix
3 large eggs
1/3 cup Crisco Oil or Puritan Oil
1 1/4 cups water
2 tablespoons brown sugar
2 tablespoons all-purpose flour
1 cup orange juice
3/4 cup dark raisins, coarsely chopped
1 envelope (1 1/4 ounces) whipped topping mix
1/4 cup flaked coconut
1/2 teaspoon grated orange peel

1. Preheat oven to 350°F. Grease and flour two 9×1½-inch round layer pans.

2. Combine dry cake mix, eggs, oil and water in large mixer bowl. Mix, bake and cool cake as directed on package.

3. For filling, combine brown sugar and flour in saucepan. Add orange juice gradually, stirring until smooth. Add raisins. Cook and stir over low heat until mixture boils and thickens, 8 to 10 minutes. Cool.

4. Spread cooled raisin filling between layers. Frost top and sides of cake with prepared whipped topping. Toss coconut with orange peel; sprinkle over top of cake.

WHITE CAKE WITH TOASTED PECAN FROSTING

12 to 16 servings

1 package Duncan Hines Deluxe White Cake Mix
3 egg whites or 3 whole eggs
1/3 cup Crisco Oil or Puritan Oil
1 1/4 cups water
1 cup coarsely chopped pecans
1/4 cup (1/2 stick) butter or margarine
1/2 cup half-and-half
1 1/2 teaspoons vanilla extract
3 1/2 cups confectioners' sugar

1. Preheat oven to 350°F. Grease and flour 13×9×2-inch pan.

2. Combine dry cake mix, egg whites or whole eggs, oil and water in large mixer bowl. Mix, bake and cool cake as directed on package.

3. For frosting, heat and stir pecans and butter in skillet over low heat until pecans are toasted. Remove from heat. Stir in half-and-half, vanilla extract and confectioners' sugar; beat until frosting is of spreading consistency. Spread over cooled cake.

CINNAMON RIPPLE CAKE

12 to 16 servings

1 package Duncan Hines Deluxe Angel Food Cake Mix
1 1/3 cups water
3 1/2 teaspoons ground cinnamon
3/4 cup whipping cream
1/2 cup cold milk
1/3 cup confectioners' sugar
1 teaspoon vanilla extract

1. Preheat oven to 375°F.

2. Prepare cake with water as directed on package. Spoon one-fourth of batter into ungreased 10-inch tube pan and spread evenly. With small fine sieve, sprinkle one teaspoon cinnamon over batter. Repeat layering two more times, ending with batter.

3. Bake at 375°F for 30 to 40 minutes or until top crust is golden brown, firm and looks very dry. Do not underbake.

4. To cool cake, hang pan upside down on bottle or funnel. When completely cooled, remove from pan.

5. To serve, beat whipping cream and milk in chilled bowl with chilled beaters until thick. Blend in confectioners' sugar, vanilla extract and remaining 1/2 teaspoon cinnamon. Cut cake into slices and top with cinnamon cream.

Raisin-Filled Orange Cake (top),
Cinnamon Ripple Cake (bottom)

CARROT CAKE SUPREME

16 to 20 servings

1 package Duncan Hines
   Deluxe Carrot Cake Mix
3 large eggs
½ cup Crisco Oil or Puritan
   Oil
½ cup water
½ cup finely chopped nuts
1 can (8 ounces) crushed
   pineapple, undrained
2 packages (3 ounces each)
   cream cheese, softened
⅓ cup butter or margarine,
   softened
1½ teaspoons vanilla extract
3½ cups confectioners' sugar
1 teaspoon milk

1. Preheat oven to 350°F. Grease and flour 13×9×2-inch pan.

2. Combine dry cake mix, eggs, oil, water, nuts and undrained pineapple in large mixer bowl. Mix cake as directed on package. Turn batter into pan and spread evenly.

3. Bake at 350°F for 35 to 40 minutes or until toothpick inserted in center comes out clean. Cool in pan on rack.

4. For cream cheese frosting*, beat cream cheese, butter and vanilla extract in bowl. Add confectioners' sugar and milk; beat until smooth and creamy. Add more confectioners' sugar to thicken or milk to thin as needed. Spread on cooled cake. Refrigerate until ready to serve.

Or in medium size bowl, mix 4 ounces softened cream cheese and 2 teaspoons lemon juice with 1 can Duncan Hines Vanilla Frosting until well blended.

EASY GERMAN CHOCOLATE CAKE

12 to 16 servings

1 package Duncan Hines
   Deluxe Swiss Chocolate
   Cake Mix
3 large eggs
½ cup Crisco Oil or Puritan
   Oil
1¼ cups water
1 cup chopped nuts
⅓ cup butter or regular
   margarine, melted
1 cup packed light brown
   sugar
1 can (3½ ounces) flaked
   coconut
¼ cup milk

1. Preheat oven to 350°F. Grease and flour 13×9×2-inch pan.

2. Combine dry cake mix, eggs, oil and water in large mixer bowl. Mix cake as directed on package. Stir in ½ cup nuts. Turn batter into pan and spread evenly.

3. Bake at 350°F for 35 to 40 minutes or until toothpick inserted in center comes out clean. Cool in pan on rack.

4. For topping, combine butter, brown sugar, coconut, milk and remaining ½ cup nuts. Spread evenly over cooled cake. Place under broiler and broil 2 to 3 minutes or until bubbly.

Easy German Chocolate Cake

New Orleans Crumb Cake

NEW ORLEANS CRUMB CAKE

16 servings

1 package Duncan Hines
  Deluxe Devil's Food Cake
  Mix
3 large eggs
½ cup Crisco Oil or Puritan
  Oil
1⅓ cups water
1 cup graham cracker
  crumbs
3 tablespoons Crisco
  shortening, melted
1 package (6 ounces)
  semisweet chocolate
  pieces (1 cup)
½ cup chopped nuts
  Sweetened whipped
  cream, if desired

1. Preheat oven to 350°F. Grease and flour 13×9×2-inch pan.

2. Combine dry cake mix, eggs, oil and water in large mixer bowl. Mix cake as directed on package. Turn batter into pan and spread evenly.

3. Combine graham cracker crumbs and melted shortening; mix well. Stir in chocolate pieces and nuts. Sprinkle evenly over batter.

4. Bake at 350°F for 40 to 50 minutes or until toothpick inserted in center comes out clean. Cool in pan on rack. Serve with whipped cream.

CRANBERRY UPSIDE-DOWN CAKE

12 to 16 servings

½ cup (1 stick) butter or
  margarine
1⅓ cups sugar
1 package (12 ounces)
  cranberries, coarsely
  chopped
1 tablespoon grated orange
  peel
1 teaspoon vanilla extract
1 package Duncan Hines
  Deluxe White Cake Mix
3 large eggs
⅓ cup Crisco Oil or
  Puritan Oil
1¼ cups water

1. Preheat oven to 350°F.

2. For topping, melt butter in 13×9×2-inch pan. Mix in 1 cup sugar; spread evenly. Mix cranberries, remaining ⅓ cup sugar, orange peel and vanilla extract. Spoon over butter-sugar mixture and spread evenly.

3. Combine dry cake mix, eggs, oil and water in large mixer bowl. Mix cake as directed on package. Turn batter into pan and spread evenly over cranberries.

4. Bake at 350°F for 40 to 50 minutes or until toothpick inserted in center comes out clean. Cool 1 to 2 minutes. Loosen cake with spatula from sides of pan and invert on large platter; remove pan after 1 to 2 minutes. Serve warm or cooled.

NUTTY CRUNCH CAKE

12 to 16 servings

1 package Duncan Hines Deluxe Carrot Cake Mix
4 large eggs
⅓ cup Crisco Oil or Puritan Oil
¾ cup water
⅓ cup all-purpose flour
¼ cup sugar
½ cup plus 1 tablespoon Jif Extra Crunchy Peanut Butter
½ cup confectioners' sugar
1 tablespoon milk
½ teaspoon vanilla extract

1. Preheat oven to 325°F. Grease and flour 8½- or 10-inch fluted tube pan.

2. Combine dry cake mix, eggs, oil and water in large mixer bowl. Mix cake as directed on package. Turn half of batter into pan and spread evenly.

3. For filling, combine flour and sugar in small bowl. Cut in ½ cup peanut butter with pastry blender until crumbly. Sprinkle filling over batter in pan. Spread remaining batter over filling.

4. Bake at 325°F for 50 to 55 minutes or until toothpick inserted in center comes out clean. Cool in pan on rack 25 minutes. Remove from pan; cool completely on rack.

5. For glaze, combine confectioners' sugar, milk, 1 tablespoon peanut butter and vanilla in small mixer bowl. Beat until smooth. Drizzle glaze over cooled cake.

SPICY APPLE CAKE

16 servings

¾ cup packed brown sugar
1 tablespoon cornstarch
½ teaspoon ground cinnamon
⅛ teaspoon ground nutmeg
⅛ teaspoon ground cloves
1 tablespoon grated orange peel
½ cup water
2 cups chopped fresh apples
1 cup raisins
¾ cup chopped walnuts
1 teaspoon vanilla extract
1 package Duncan Hines Deluxe Spice Cake Mix
3 large eggs
⅓ cup Crisco Oil or Puritan Oil
1¼ cups water
Whipped cream, ice cream or hard sauce, if desired

1. Preheat oven to 350°F. Grease 13×9×2-inch pan and line with waxed paper; grease paper.

2. Combine brown sugar, cornstarch, cinnamon, nutmeg, cloves, orange peel and ½ cup water in saucepan. Cook and stir over medium heat until mixture boils and thickens. Remove from heat; stir in apples, raisins, walnuts and vanilla extract. Turn into pan and spread evenly.

3. Combine dry cake mix, eggs, oil and 1¼ cups water in large mixer bowl. Mix batter as directed on package. Turn into pan and spread evenly over apple mixture.

4. Bake at 350°F for 40 to 45 minutes or until toothpick inserted in center comes out clean. At once, invert pan onto large platter. Remove pan and peel off paper. Serve warm with whipped cream, ice cream or hard sauce, if desired.

CARAMEL ANGEL FINGERS

24 slices

1 package Duncan Hines Deluxe Angel Food Cake Mix
1⅓ cups water
½ cup (1 stick) butter or margarine
¼ cup milk
1 cup packed brown sugar
1¾ cups confectioners' sugar
1 cup chopped salted peanuts

1. Preheat oven to 350°F. Line 15½×10½×1-inch jelly roll pan with aluminum foil allowing foil to extend about 1 inch above rim of pan.

2. Prepare cake with water as directed on package. Turn batter into lined pan and spread evenly. Cut through batter with knife or spatula to remove large air bubbles. Bake at 350°F for 28 to 33 minutes or until top springs back when lightly touched with fingertip. At once turn cake onto large tray. Gently peel off foil and allow cake to cool.

3. For frosting, heat butter, milk and brown sugar in saucepan; stir until sugar is dissolved. Stir in confectioners' sugar. Remove from heat. Beat until frosting is of spreading consistency; adding more confectioners' sugar, if necessary. Spread over cooled cake and sprinkle with peanuts. Cut into finger-like slices.

Nutty Crunch Cake (top),
Caramel Angel Fingers (bottom)

Cherry Nut Cake

CHERRY NUT CAKE

12 to 16 servings

1 package Duncan Hines Deluxe Cherry Cake Mix
1 package (4-serving-size) vanilla instant pudding and pie filling mix
1¼ cups buttermilk
4 large eggs
½ cup Crisco Oil or Puritan Oil
1 cup flaked coconut
1 cup finely chopped pecans
Confectioners' sugar

1. Preheat oven to 350°F. Grease and flour 10-inch fluted tube pan.

2. Combine dry cake mix, instant pudding mix, buttermilk, eggs and oil in large mixer bowl. Mix cake as directed on package. Stir in coconut and pecans. Turn batter into pan and spread evenly.

3. Bake at 350°F for 50 to 60 minutes or until toothpick inserted in center comes out clean. Cool in pan on rack 1 hour. Remove cake from pan and let stand overnight before serving.

4. To serve, sift confectioners' sugar over top of cake.

PRALINE BUTTER CAKE

16 to 20 servings

1 package Duncan Hines Butter Recipe Golden or Fudge Cake Mix
3 large eggs
½ cup (1 stick) butter or margarine, softened
⅔ cup water
6 tablespoons butter or margarine, softened
1 cup packed light brown sugar
½ cup undiluted evaporated milk
1 teaspoon vanilla extract
1 cup flaked coconut
1 cup chopped pecans

1. Preheat oven to 375°F. Grease and flour 13×9×2-inch pan.

2. Combine dry cake mix, eggs, ½ cup butter and water in large mixer bowl. Mix and bake cake as directed on package. Set pan on rack. Preheat broiler.

3. For topping, combine 6 tablespoons butter and brown sugar in bowl. Stir in evaporated milk and vanilla extract; blend well. Stir in coconut and pecans. Spread over cake in pan. Place cake under broiler and broil for 3 to 5 minutes or until topping is brown.

GLAZED CHOCOLATE LOAVES

24 to 32 servings

1 package Duncan Hines
  Deluxe Sour Cream
  Chocolate Cake Mix
1 cup quick-cooking oats
3 large eggs
½ cup Crisco Oil or
  Puritan Oil
1¼ cups water
2 tablespoons butter or
  margarine
⅓ cup packed brown sugar
2 tablespoons milk
1 cup confectioners' sugar
1 teaspoon vanilla extract

1. Preheat oven to 350°F. Grease and flour two 8½×4½×2½-inch loaf pans.

2. Combine dry cake mix and oats in large mixer bowl. Add eggs, oil and water; blend, then beat 2 minutes at medium speed. Divide batter evenly in pans.

3. Bake at 350°F for 35 to 40 minutes or until toothpick inserted in centers comes out clean. Cool in pans on racks 10 minutes. Remove from pans; cool completely on racks.

4. For glaze, combine butter, brown sugar and milk in small saucepan. Cook over low heat, stirring occasionally, until butter is melted. Remove from heat. Stir in confectioners' sugar and vanilla extract. Beat until frosting is smooth and of spreading consistency. Spread over tops of cooled cakes.

PEANUT BUTTER ANGEL ROLL

12 to 16 servings

1 package Duncan Hines
  Deluxe Angel Food Cake
  Mix
1⅓ cups water
¼ cup confectioners' sugar
1 cup Jif Peanut Butter
½ cup chopped peanuts
3 tablespoons orange
  marmalade
3 tablespoons honey
1½ cups confectioners' sugar
2 tablespoons orange juice

1. Preheat oven to 350°F. Line 15½×10½×1-inch jelly-roll pan with foil allowing foil to extend 1 inch above rim of pan.

2. Prepare cake with water as directed on package. Turn batter into foil-lined pan and spread evenly. Cut through batter with knife or spatula to remove large air bubbles.

3. Bake at 350°F for 30 minutes or until top springs back when lightly touched with fingertip. At once turn cake out onto towel covered with ¼ cup confectioners' sugar. Gently peel off foil. Roll up cake, starting at narrow end, rolling up towel with cake. Cool on rack.

4. For filling, combine peanut butter, peanuts, orange marmalade and honey; mix well. Unroll cake and spread entire surface with filling; reroll.

5. For glaze, combine 1½ cups confectioners' sugar and orange juice. Beat until smooth. Drizzle glaze over cake.

Peanut Butter Angel Roll

GERMAN CHOCOLATE CAKE

1 package Duncan Hines Deluxe Swiss Chocolate Cake Mix
3 large eggs
½ cup Crisco Oil or Puritan Oil
1¼ cups water
⅔ cup sugar
⅔ cup undiluted evaporated milk
2 egg yolks
⅓ cup Crisco shortening
1 can (3½ ounces) flaked coconut
1 cup chopped pecans
½ teaspoon vanilla extract

1. Preheat oven to 350°F. Grease and flour two 8×1½ or 9×1½-inch round layer pans.

2. Combine dry cake mix, eggs, oil and water in large mixer bowl. Mix, bake and cool cake as directed on package.

3. For frosting, combine sugar, evaporated milk, egg yolks and shortening in saucepan. Cook and stir over medium heat until mixture boils. Remove from heat. Add coconut, pecans and vanilla extract. Beat until thick. Cool 15 minutes. Spread between cooled layers and on top of cake.

FRENCH APPLE CAKE

3 cooking apples, pared, cored and sliced (about 3 cups)
⅔ cup sugar
1 tablespoon all-purpose flour
½ teaspoon ground cinnamon
2 tablespoons butter or margarine, melted
2 tablespoons lemon juice
1 package Duncan Hines Deluxe White Cake Mix
3 large eggs
⅓ cup Crisco Oil or Puritan Oil
1¼ cups water

1. Preheat oven to 350°F. Grease 13×9×2-inch pan.

2. Arrange apples in pan. Mix sugar, flour and cinnamon; sprinkle over apples. Combine melted butter and lemon juice; drizzle over apples.

3. Place dry cake mix, eggs, oil and water in large mixer bowl. Mix cake as directed on package. Turn batter into pan over apples and spread evenly.

4. Bake at 350°F for 40 to 50 minutes or until toothpick inserted in center comes out clean. Cool 1 to 2 minutes in pan. Invert on large platter or tray; remove pan after 1 to 2 minutes. Serve warm.

French Apple Cake

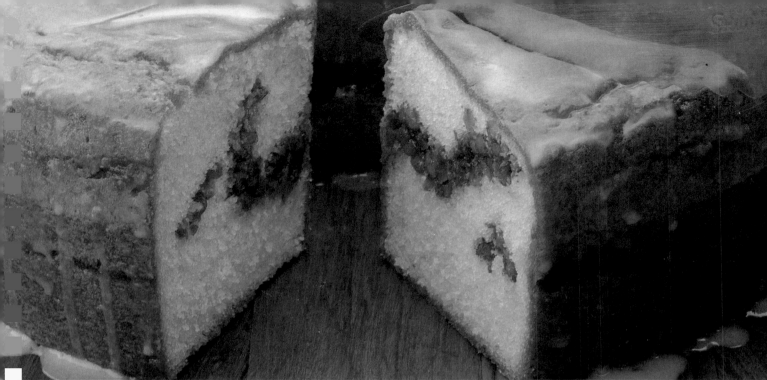

SOCK-IT-TO-ME CAKE

12 to 16 servings

1 package Duncan Hines
  Butter Recipe Golden
  Cake Mix
1 cup finely chopped pecans
2 tablespoons brown sugar
2 teaspoons ground
  cinnamon
1 cup dairy sour cream
⅓ cup Crisco Oil or Puritan
  Oil
¼ cup sugar
¼ cup water
4 large eggs
1 cup confectioners' sugar
2 tablespoons milk

1. Preheat oven to 375°F. Grease and flour 10-inch tube pan.

2. For filling, combine 2 tablespoons cake mix, pecans, brown sugar and cinnamon; mix well. Set aside.

3. Combine remaining dry cake mix, sour cream, oil, sugar, water and eggs in large mixer bowl. Beat 2 minutes at high speed. Turn two-thirds of batter into pan; sprinkle with filling. Spoon remaining batter evenly over filling mixture.

4. Bake at 375°F for 45 to 55 minutes or until toothpick inserted in center comes out clean. Cool in pan on rack 25 minutes; remove from pan.

5. For glaze*, blend together confectioners' sugar and milk; drizzle over warm cake.

Or heat ⅔ cup Duncan Hines Vanilla Frosting in small saucepan over medium heat, stirring constantly, until thin.

PEANUT BUTTER SUNDAE CAKE

24 servings

1 package Duncan Hines
  Deluxe Yellow Cake Mix
3 large eggs
¼ cup Crisco Oil or
  Puritan Oil
1¼ cups water
6 tablespoons Jif Creamy
  Peanut Butter, divided
1 can (14 ounces)
  sweetened condensed milk
1 quart vanilla ice cream

1. Preheat oven to 350°F. Grease and flour 15½×10½×1-inch jelly roll pan.

2. Combine dry cake mix, eggs, oil, water and 4 tablespoons peanut butter in large mixer bowl. Prepare cake as directed on package. Turn batter into pan and spread evenly.

3. Bake at 350°F for 30 to 35 minutes or until toothpick inserted in center comes out clean. Cool cake in pan on rack.

4. For peanut butter sauce, combine sweetened condensed milk and 2 tablespoons peanut butter in small saucepan. Cook and stir over low heat for 5 minutes. Cool completely. Refrigerate 1 hour or until slightly thickened.

5. To serve, cut cake into squares and top with ice cream and peanut butter sauce.

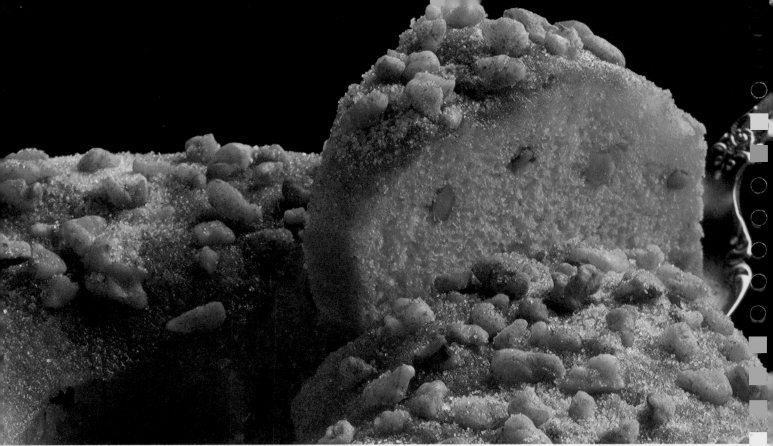

Orange Cinnamon Tea Cake

ORANGE CINNAMON TEA CAKE

16 servings

1 package Duncan Hines
    Deluxe Orange Cake Mix
3 large eggs
⅓ cup Crisco Oil or Puritan
    Oil
1¼ cups water
½ cup plus ⅓ cup chopped
    walnuts
⅓ cup orange juice
⅓ cup sugar
1 teaspoon ground
    cinnamon

1. Preheat oven to 350°F. Grease and flour 10-inch tube pan.

2. Combine dry cake mix, eggs, oil and water in large mixer bowl. Mix cake as directed on package; stir in ½ cup chopped walnuts. Turn batter into pan and spread evenly.

3. Bake at 350°F for 45 to 55 minutes or until toothpick inserted in center comes out clean. Cool in pan on rack 25 minutes, then remove from pan.

4. Pour orange juice over warm cake and immediately sprinkle with mixture of sugar, cinnamon and remaining ⅓ cup chopped walnuts.

CHOCOLATE MALTED CAKE

12 to 16 servings

1 package Duncan Hines
    Deluxe Swiss Chocolate
    Cake Mix
4 large eggs
½ cup Crisco Oil or
    Puritan Oil
1¼ cups water
1¼ cups instant malted milk
    powder, divided
½ cup Crisco shortening
¼ cup unsweetened cocoa
¼ teaspoon salt
4 cups confectioners' sugar
⅓ cup milk
1 teaspoon vanilla extract

1. Preheat oven to 350°F. Grease and flour two 9×1½-inch round layer pans.

2. Combine dry cake mix, 3 eggs, oil, water and ¾ cup malted milk powder in large mixer bowl. Mix cake as directed on package. Divide batter evenly in pans.

3. Bake at 350°F for 30 to 35 minutes or until toothpick inserted in center comes out clean. Cool in pans on racks 10 minutes. Remove from pans; cool completely on racks.

4. For chocolate malted frosting, blend shortening, 1 egg, ½ cup malted milk powder, cocoa and salt in bowl. Add confectioners' sugar alternately with milk and vanilla extract, mixing until smooth and creamy. Add more confectioners' sugar to thicken or milk to thin as needed. Spread between cooled layers and on sides and top of cake.

LEMON ANGEL FOOD CAKE

12 to 16 servings

1 package Duncan Hines
Deluxe Angel Food
Cake Mix
1 cup plus 3 tablespoons
water
2 tablespoons lemon juice
Few drops yellow food
coloring
1 teaspoon grated lemon
peel*

1. Preheat oven to 375°F.

2. Prepare cake mix as directed on package using combined water, lemon juice and yellow food coloring instead of 1⅓ cups water. Add grated lemon peel along with cake flour mixture (red "B" packet). Pour batter into ungreased 10-inch tube pan. Cut through batter with knife or spatula to remove large air bubbles.

3. Bake at 375°F for 30 to 40 minutes or until top crust is golden brown, firm and dry. Do not underbake. To cool, hang pan upside-down on funnel or bottle at least 1½ hours. Remove from pan.

For stronger lemon flavor, add more lemon peel.

CHOCOLATE CREAM TORTE

12 to 16 servings

1 package Duncan Hines
Deluxe Devil's Food
Cake Mix
3 large eggs
½ cup Crisco Oil or
Puritan Oil
1⅓ cups water
2 cups whipping cream
¼ cup sugar
1 teaspoon vanilla extract
1 cup finely chopped
walnuts
Walnut halves, if desired

1. Preheat oven to 350°F. Grease and flour two 8 × 1½ or 9 × 1½-inch round layer pans.

2. Combine dry cake mix, eggs, oil and water in large mixer bowl. Mix, bake and cool cake as directed on package. Refrigerate layers for ease in splitting.

3. Whip cream until soft peaks form. Beat in sugar and vanilla extract. Fold in chopped walnuts. Split each layer into two thin layers. Spread whipped cream mixture between layers and on sides and top of cake. Refrigerate until ready to serve. Garnish with walnut halves, if desired. Store leftover cake in refrigerator.

Chocolate Cream Torte

RHUBARB-SAUCED STRAWBERRY CAKE

15 servings

1   package Duncan Hines
    Deluxe Strawberry Cake
    Mix
¾   cup water
½   cup orange juice
3   large eggs
⅓   cup Crisco Oil or Puritan
    Oil
6   cups sliced rhubarb
2   cups sugar
½   teaspoon grated orange
    peel
¼   teaspoon ground
    cinnamon
¼   teaspoon ground nutmeg

1. Preheat oven to 350°F. Grease and flour 15½ × 10½ × 1-inch jelly-roll pan.

2. Place dry cake mix, water, orange juice, eggs and oil in large mixer bowl. Mix cake as directed on package. Turn batter into pan and spread evenly.

3. Bake at 350°F for 25 to 30 minutes or until toothpick inserted in center comes out clean. Cool in pan on rack.

4. For rhubarb sauce, combine rhubarb, sugar, orange peel, cinnamon and nutmeg in 2-quart saucepan. Cook over high heat until mixture boils; reduce heat to low and simmer, covered, 5 to 7 minutes or until rhubarb is tender; cool. To serve, cut cake into squares and spoon sauce over cake.

LEMON SUPREME POUND CAKE

12 to 16 servings

1   package Duncan Hines
    Deluxe Lemon Cake Mix
4   large eggs
⅓   cup Crisco Oil or
    Puritan Oil
1   cup water
1   package (4-serving-size)
    lemon instant pudding and
    pie filling mix
1   cup confectioners' sugar
2   tablespoons milk or 2
    tablespoons lemon juice

1. Preheat oven to 350°F. Grease and flour 10-inch tube pan.

2. Combine dry cake mix, eggs, oil, water and pudding mix in large mixer bowl. Mix batter as directed on package. Turn batter into pan and spread evenly.

3. Bake at 350°F for 50 to 60 minutes or until toothpick inserted in center comes out clean. Cool in pan on rack 25 minutes; remove from pan.

4. For glaze*, blend together confectioners' sugar and milk; drizzle over warm cake. Cool completely on rack.

Or combine ⅔ cup Duncan Hines Vanilla Frosting and 1 teaspoon lemon juice in small saucepan; heat over medium heat, stirring constantly until thin.

CHOCOLATE ZUCCHINI CAKE

12 to 16 servings

1 package Duncan Hines
   Deluxe Deep Chocolate
   Cake Mix
1 teaspoon ground
   cinnamon
3 large eggs
½ cup Crisco Oil or Puritan
   Oil
1¼ cups water
1 cup shredded, unpared
   zucchini
2 packages (3 ounces each)
   cream cheese, softened
⅓ cup butter or margarine,
   softened
1½ teaspoons vanilla extract
3½ cups confectioners' sugar
1 teaspoon milk
¼ cup chopped nuts

1. Preheat oven to 350°F. Grease and flour 10-inch tube pan.

2. Combine dry cake mix and cinnamon in large mixer bowl. Add eggs, oil and water; blend, then beat 2 minutes at medium speed; fold in zucchini. Turn batter into pan and spread evenly.

3. Bake at 350°F for 50 to 60 minutes or until toothpick inserted in center comes out clean. Cool in pan on rack 25 minutes. Remove from pan; cool completely on rack.

4. For frosting*, beat cream cheese, butter, and vanilla in bowl. Add confectioners' sugar and milk; mix until creamy. Add confectioners' sugar to thicken or milk to thin as needed. Spread on cooled cake. Sprinkle with nuts. Refrigerate until ready to serve.

Or in medium size bowl, mix 4 ounces softened cream cheese and 2 teaspoons lemon juice with 1 can Duncan Hines Vanilla Frosting until well blended.

NEAPOLITAN REFRIGERATOR SHEET CAKE

16 to 20 servings

1 package (3 ounces)
   strawberry-flavored
   gelatin
¾ cup boiling water
½ cup cold water
1 package Duncan Hines
   Deluxe Fudge Marble
   Cake Mix
3 large eggs
⅓ cup Crisco Oil or
   Puritan Oil
1¼ cups water
1 envelope (1¼ ounces)
   whipped topping mix
1 package (4-serving-size)
   vanilla instant pudding
   and pie filling mix
1½ cups cold milk
1 teaspoon vanilla extract
   Fresh strawberries, if
   desired

1. Preheat oven to 350°F. Grease and flour 13×9×2-inch pan.

2. Dissolve gelatin in boiling water. Stir in ½ cup cold water; set aside at room temperature.

3. Prepare and bake cake as directed on package using eggs, oil and 1¼ cups water. Cool in pan on rack 20 to 25 minutes.

4. Poke deep holes through top of cake with meat fork, spacing holes about 1 inch apart. Slowly pour gelatin mixture over cooled cake. Refrigerate while preparing topping.

5. For topping, blend topping mix, instant pudding mix, cold milk and vanilla extract in chilled deep bowl. Beat until stiff, 3 to 8 minutes. Immediately spread on cake. Refrigerate until well chilled. Decorate with fresh strawberries, if desired.

Note: Cake must be stored in refrigerator and served chilled. Frosted cake can be frozen.

MOCHA CHOCOLATE CHIP RING

12 to 16 servings

1 package Duncan Hines
   Deluxe Chocolate Chip
   Cake Mix
1 cup plus 4 teaspoons cold
   coffee, divided
3 large eggs
⅓ cup Crisco Oil or
   Puritan Oil
1 cup confectioners' sugar

1. Preheat oven to 350°F. Grease and flour 10-inch fluted tube pan.

2. Combine dry cake mix, 1 cup coffee, eggs and oil in large mixer bowl. Mix cake as directed on package. Turn into pan and spread evenly.

3. Bake at 350°F for 45 to 55 minutes or until toothpick inserted in center comes out clean. Cool in pan on rack 25 minutes. Remove from pan and cool completely on rack.

4. For glaze, mix confectioners' sugar and 4 teaspoons cold coffee until smooth; drizzle over cooled cake.

Cookies & Bars

WHEAT GERM COOKIES

About 3 dozen cookies

1 package Duncan Hines
  Deluxe Yellow Cake Mix
1 large egg
3 tablespoons brown sugar
¼ cup Crisco Oil or Puritan
  Oil
2 tablespoons butter or
  margarine, melted
½ cup wheat germ
2 tablespoons water
½ cup chopped nuts

1. Preheat oven to 375°F.

2. Combine dry cake mix, egg, brown sugar, oil, butter, wheat germ and water in bowl. Mix with spoon. (Dough will be stiff.) Stir in nuts.

3. Drop by teaspoonfuls, 2 inches apart, on ungreased cookie sheets.

4. Bake at 375°F for 10 minutes for chewy cookies, 12 minutes for crispy cookies. Cool 1 minute on cookie sheet, then remove to rack to finish cooling.

CHEWY APPLE 'N' FRUIT BARS

2½ dozen bars

1 package Duncan Hines
  Deluxe Apple Cake Mix
1 cup chopped mixed dried
  fruit
2 large eggs
½ cup Crisco Oil or
  Puritan Oil

1. Preheat oven to 350°F. Grease 15½×10½×1-inch jelly roll pan.

2. Combine dry cake mix, dried fruit, eggs and oil in large bowl. Stir until well mixed. Turn mixture into pan and spread evenly.

3. Bake at 350°F for 15 to 20 minutes or until set and lightly browned at edges. Cool on rack. Cut into bars.

CARROT BARS

2 dozen bars

1 package Duncan Hines
  Deluxe Carrot Cake Mix
3 large eggs
⅔ cup Crisco Oil or
  Puritan Oil
1 cup chopped nuts
1 cup raisins

1. Preheat oven to 350°F. Grease and flour 13×9×2-inch pan.

2. Combine dry cake mix, eggs and oil in large mixer bowl; mix well. Stir in nuts and raisins. Spread evenly in pan.

3. Bake at 350°F for 25 to 30 minutes or until toothpick inserted in center comes out clean. Cool in pan on rack. Cut into bars.

Wheat Germ Cookies

REFRIGERATOR NUT WAFERS

7 dozen cookies

1 package Duncan Hines
  Deluxe Yellow Cake Mix
1 large egg
½ cup Crisco Oil or
  Puritan Oil
2 tablespoons water
1 teaspoon vanilla extract
1 cup chopped nuts

1. Mix together dry cake mix, egg, oil, water and vanilla extract in bowl. Work in nuts with your hands. Shape dough into two 2-inch diameter rolls. Wrap in waxed paper and refrigerate 8 hours or overnight.

2. Preheat oven to 375°F.

3. Slice dough very thinly and place on ungreased cookie sheets.

4. Bake at 375°F for 6 to 8 minutes or until light golden brown.

FROSTED COOKIES

About 4 dozen cookies

1 package Duncan Hines
  Deluxe Fudge Marble
  Cake Mix
⅓ cup Crisco Oil or Puritan
  Oil
1 teaspoon ground ginger
2 large eggs
⅓ cup Crisco shortening
⅓ cup water
½ teaspoon salt
3 cups confectioners' sugar
1 teaspoon vanilla extract
  Milk
  Chopped nuts or coconut,
  if desired

1. Preheat oven to 350°F.

2. Combine dry cake mix, oil, ginger and eggs in bowl (do not add contents of small packet); mix well. Drop dough by teaspoonfuls onto ungreased cookie sheets.

3. Bake at 350°F for 12 to 15 minutes. Cool about 1 minute on cookie sheet, then remove to rack to finish cooling.

4. For frosting, heat shortening, water, salt and contents of small packet in saucepan until shortening melts. Remove from heat. Add confectioners' sugar and vanilla extract; beat until smooth and creamy. Add more confectioners' sugar to thicken or milk to thin as needed. Spread on cooled cookies. Sprinkle with chopped nuts or coconut.

RIBBON COOKIES

About 6 dozen cookies

2 large eggs
¼ teaspoon baking soda
½ cup Crisco shortening
1 package Duncan Hines
  Deluxe Fudge Marble
  Cake Mix
¼ cup all-purpose flour

1. Beat eggs with baking soda in bowl. Add shortening. Blend in dry cake mix and flour; mix well (do not add contents of small packet). Divide dough in half. Blend contents of small packet into one half of dough.

2. On wax paper, shape each half of dough into a long strip ½ inch thick and 1½ inches wide. Press strips together lightly. Cut to make three short strips. Wrap in wax paper and refrigerate.

3. Preheat oven to 350°F.

4. Slice dough ¼ inch thick and place on ungreased cookie sheets.

5. Bake at 350°F for 10 minutes. Cool about 1 minute on cookie sheets; remove to rack to finish cooling.

COCONUT CHOCOLATE CHIP BARS

2½ dozen bars

1 package Duncan Hines
  Deluxe Chocolate Chip
  Cake Mix
1 cup flaked coconut
2 large eggs
½ cup Crisco Oil or
  Puritan Oil

1. Preheat oven to 350°F. Grease 15½×10½×1-inch jelly roll pan.

2. Combine dry cake mix, coconut, eggs and oil in large bowl. Mix until blended. Turn mixture into pan and spread evenly.

3. Bake at 350°F for 15 to 20 minutes or until set and lightly browned at edges. Cool in pan on rack. Cut into bars.

RASPBERRY OATMEAL BARS

1 package Duncan Hines
   Deluxe Yellow Cake Mix
2½ cups quick-cooking oats
¾ cup (1½ sticks) butter or
   margarine, melted
1 cup (12-ounce jar)
   raspberry preserves or
   jam*
1 tablespoon water

1. Preheat oven to 375°F. Grease 13×9×2-inch pan.

2. Combine dry cake mix and oats in large bowl; add melted butter and stir until crumbly. Measure half of crumb mixture (about 3 cups) into pan. Press firmly to cover bottom. Combine preserves and water; stir until blended. Spread over crumb mixture in pan. Sprinkle remaining crumb mixture over preserves; pat firmly to make top even.

3. Bake at 375°F for 18 to 23 minutes or until top is very light brown. Cool in pan on rack; cut into bars. Store in airtight container.

*Apricot, blackberry or strawberry preserves can be substituted.

COCONUT MALLOW FUDGE SQUARES

About 4 dozen squares

1 package Duncan Hines
  Deluxe Devil's Food Cake
  Mix
½ cup quick-cooking oats
1 large egg, slightly beaten
½ cup Crisco Oil or Puritan
  Oil
1 package (6 ounces)
  semisweet chocolate
  pieces (1 cup)
1 package (6 ounces)
  butterscotch-flavored
  pieces (1 cup)
3 cups miniature
  marshmallows
1 cup flaked coconut

1. Preheat oven to 350°F. Grease 15½×10½×1-inch jelly roll pan.

2. Combine dry cake mix, oats, egg and oil in bowl. Mix with spoon until dry ingredients are completely moistened. Press mixture firmly and evenly into pan.

3. Bake at 350°F for 10 minutes. Remove from oven. Sprinkle chocolate pieces over crust, then butterscotch pieces, marshmallows and coconut. Bake 15 minutes more or until coconut and marshmallows just begin to brown. Cool on rack; cut into squares.

CARAMEL CHOCOLATE FINGERS

About 3 dozen bars

1 package (14 ounces)
  vanilla caramels
⅔ cup evaporated milk
1 package Duncan Hines
  Deluxe Swiss Chocolate
  Cake Mix
¾ cup (1½ sticks) butter or
  margarine, melted
1 package (6 ounces)
  semisweet chocolate
  pieces (1 cup)

1. Preheat oven to 350°F. Grease 13×9×2-inch pan.

2. Combine caramels and ⅓ cup evaporated milk in heavy saucepan. Heat and stir until blended; keep warm.

3. Combine dry cake mix, melted butter and ⅓ cup evaporated milk in bowl; mix well. Spread half of mixture in bottom of pan.

4. Bake at 350°F for 6 minutes.

5. Immediately sprinkle chocolate over hot layer; drizzle with caramel mixture. Spread remaining batter evenly over top.

6. Return to oven and bake 15 to 18 minutes more or until top looks dry. Cool on rack; cut into fingers, about 3×1 inch.

DOUBLE CHOCOLATE CHEWIES

3 dozen bars

1 package Duncan Hines
  Deluxe Deep Chocolate
  Cake Mix
2 large eggs
¼ cup Crisco Oil or
  Puritan Oil
1 package (6 ounces)
  semisweet chocolate
  pieces (1 cup)
1 cup chopped nuts

1. Preheat oven to 350°F. Grease 13×9×2-inch baking pan.

2. Combine dry cake mix, eggs and oil in bowl; mix well (mixture will be stiff). Stir in chocolate pieces and nuts, using your hands, if necessary. Pat mixture into even layer in pan.

3. Bake at 350°F for 20 to 25 minutes. Cool in pan on rack. Cut into bars.

Creamy Carrot Cheese Squares

CREAMY CARROT CHEESE SQUARES

About 20 squares

1 package Duncan Hines
Deluxe Carrot Cake Mix
½ cup (1 stick) butter or
margarine, melted
1 cup chopped pecans
2 packages (8 ounces each)
cream cheese, softened
2 large eggs
1 teaspoon vanilla extract
20 pecan halves

1. Preheat oven to 350°F. Grease and flour 13×9×2-inch pan. Measure 1½ cups dry cake mix; set aside.

2. Combine remaining cake mix and melted butter in large mixer bowl. Mix at low speed until crumbly. Stir in chopped pecans. Press firmly into pan.

3. Bake at 350°F for 6 minutes. Cool 5 minutes, then set pan in freezer for 5 minutes or until bottom of pan is cold.

4. Beat cream cheese in large mixer bowl until smooth. Beat in reserved 1½ cups cake mix, eggs and vanilla extract. Spread over cooled crust. Arrange pecan halves on top.

5. Bake at 350°F for 23 to 28 minutes or until toothpick inserted in center comes out clean. Cool on rack. Cut into bars. Store in refrigerator.

SUGAR COOKIES

5 to 6 dozen cookies

1 package Duncan Hines
Deluxe Yellow or White
Cake Mix
¾ cup Crisco shortening,
melted and cooled
1 large egg
2 tablespoons milk

1. Combine all ingredients in bowl; mix well. Refrigerate at least 2 hours.

2. Preheat oven to 375°F. Roll out chilled dough ⅛ to ¼ inch thick on lightly floured surface. Cut into desired shapes with floured cookie cutters. Decorate as desired.

3. Bake at 375°F for 6 to 10 minutes or until edges start to brown. Cool several minutes on cookie sheet, then remove to rack to finish cooling. Store in airtight container.

CANDY BAR COOKIES

About 4 dozen small bars

1 package Duncan Hines
  Deluxe Yellow Cake Mix
½ cup Crisco Oil or Puritan
  Oil
1 large egg
1 package (14 ounces)
  vanilla caramels
⅓ cup evaporated milk
⅓ cup butter or margarine
1⅔ cups confectioners' sugar
1 cup chopped pecans
1 package (6 ounces)
  semisweet chocolate
  pieces (1 cup)

1. Preheat oven to 350°F.

2. For crust, combine dry cake mix, oil and egg in bowl with pastry blender. Spread evenly over bottom of ungreased 13×9×2-inch pan.

3. Bake at 350°F for 15 to 20 minutes or until light golden brown. Prepare filling while crust is baking.

4. Combine caramels and evaporated milk in top of double boiler; heat until caramels melt, stirring occasionally. Add butter; stir until melted. Remove from heat. Stir in confectioners' sugar and pecans. Spread hot caramel mixture over warm, baked crust.

5. Melt semisweet chocolate pieces over hot water in top of double boiler. Spread in very thin layer over caramel filling. Refrigerate; cut into bars when cool.

GLAZED NUT BARS

About 4 dozen bars

1 package Duncan Hines
  Deluxe White Cake Mix
½ cup water
2 large eggs
¼ cup (½ stick) butter or
  margarine, softened
¼ cup packed brown sugar
1 package (6 ounces)
  semisweet chocolate
  pieces (1 cup)
½ cup chopped nuts

1. Preheat oven to 375°F. Grease and flour 13×9×2-inch pan.

2. Place dry cake mix, ¼ cup water, eggs, butter and brown sugar in large bowl. Mix thoroughly (batter will be thick). Stir in ¾ cup chocolate pieces and nuts. Turn batter into pan and spread evenly.

3. Bake at 375°F for 25 to 30 minutes or until toothpick inserted in center comes out clean. Set pan on rack.

4. Melt remaining ¼ cup chocolate pieces and remaining ¼ cup water in small saucepan. Simmer 3 minutes. Spread over warm, baked layer. Cool on rack. Cut into bars. Store in airtight container.

RAISIN BARS

2½ dozen bars

1 package Duncan Hines
  Deluxe Lemon Cake Mix
3 large eggs
⅓ cup Crisco Oil or
  Puritan Oil
1¼ cups water
1½ cups raisins
1½ cups boiling water
½ cup sugar
3 tablespoons all-purpose
  flour
½ cup finely chopped
  walnuts
1 tablespoon lemon juice

1. Preheat oven to 350°F. Grease and flour 15½×10½×1-inch jelly roll pan.

2. Combine dry cake mix, eggs, oil and 1¼ cups water in large mixer bowl. Mix as directed on package. Turn batter into pan and spread evenly.

3. Bake at 350°F for 30 to 35 minutes or until toothpick inserted in center comes out clean. Cool in pan on rack.

4. For topping, combine raisins and 1½ cups boiling water in small saucepan. Boil 5 minutes or until raisins are plump. Combine sugar and flour; stir into raisin mixture. Cook 4 minutes or until thickened. Stir in walnuts and lemon juice. Spread hot topping over bars. Cool in pan on rack. Cut into bars.

LEMON BARS

2 ½ dozen bars

1   package Duncan Hines
    Deluxe Lemon Cake Mix
3   large eggs
⅓   cup Crisco shortening
½   cup sugar
½   teaspoon baking powder
¼   teaspoon salt
2   teaspoons grated lemon
    peel
¼   cup lemon juice
    Confectioners' sugar

1. Preheat oven to 350°F.

2. Combine dry cake mix, 1 egg and shortening in bowl; mix until crumbly. Measure 1 cup and set aside. Pat remaining mixture lightly in ungreased 13×9×2-inch pan.

3. Bake at 350°F for 15 minutes or until light brown.

4. Beat remaining two eggs, sugar, baking powder, salt, lemon peel and lemon juice until light and foamy. Pour over hot crust; sprinkle with reserved 1 cup crumb mixture.

5. Bake at 350°F for 15 minutes or until light brown. Sprinkle with confectioners' sugar. Cool on rack; cut into bars.

Elegant Cakes & Tortes

LUSCIOUS CHOCOLATE PARTY CAKE

16 servings

1 package Duncan Hines Deluxe Devil's Food Cake Mix
3 large eggs
½ cup Crisco Oil or Puritan Oil
1⅓ cups water
2 ounces (2 squares) unsweetened chocolate
½ cup plus 2 tablespoons sugar
2 tablespoons water
4 large egg yolks, slightly beaten
2 tablespoons rum
1 cup (2 sticks) butter or margarine, softened
2 cups confectioners' sugar
4 large egg whites
1 cup whipping cream
½ teaspoon vanilla extract
 Chocolate curls
 Red maraschino cherries

1. Preheat oven to 350°F. Grease and flour two 8×1½-inch round layer pans.

2. Combine dry cake mix, 3 eggs, oil and 1⅓ cups water in large mixer bowl. Mix, bake and cool cake as directed on package. Chill cooled layers to make splitting easier. Split each cake layer into two thin layers.

3. Combine chocolate, ¼ cup sugar and 2 tablespoons water in top of double boiler. Heat over hot water until chocolate melts. Stir to blend, then stir a little hot mixture into 4 yolks. Return yolk mixture to double boiler top. Cook and stir until thick and smooth, about 3 minutes. Remove from heat. Cool.

4. Stir rum into cooled chocolate mixture. Cream butter and confectioners' sugar until light and fluffy. Fold in chocolate mixture. Beat 4 egg whites until frothy. Gradually add ¼ cup sugar, beating until stiff peaks form. Fold in chocolate mixture. Refrigerate 1 hour or until firm enough to spread. Spread between layers and on sides of cake. Do not spread over top layer. Refrigerate overnight or until firm.

5. To serve, whip cream until stiff. Fold in remaining 2 tablespoons sugar and vanilla extract. Spread over top of cake. Decorate with chocolate curls and maraschino cherries. Store in refrigerator.

CALYPSO CAKE

12 to 16 servings

1 package Duncan Hines Deluxe Yellow Cake Mix
3 large eggs
⅓ cup Crisco Oil or Puritan Oil
1¼ cups water
1 package (8 ounces) plus 1 package (3 ounces) cream cheese, softened
⅔ cup sugar
¼ teaspoon ground nutmeg
2 tablespoons milk
3 fresh medium peaches, peeled and diced (about 1½ cups)*
 Peeled fresh peach slices, if desired

1. Preheat oven to 350°F. Grease and flour two 8×1½ or 9×1½-inch round layer pans.

2. Combine dry cake mix, eggs, oil and water in large mixer bowl. Mix, bake and cool cake as directed on package. Refrigerate one cooled layer for ease in splitting. Split chilled layer into two thin layers.

3. For frosting, combine cream cheese, sugar, nutmeg and milk in bowl. Beat until smooth. Put about two-thirds of the mixture in another bowl; fold in diced peaches.

4. Spread half of peach mixture on top of one thin layer; place unsplit layer on top and spread with remaining peach mixture. Top with remaining thin layer. Frost top with plain cream cheese mixture. Refrigerate until ready to serve. Just before serving, garnish with sliced peaches, if desired. Store leftover cake in refrigerator.

*Apricots or melon can be substituted for peaches.

Luscious Chocolate Party Cake

OPEN HOUSE RIBBON TORTE

12 to 16 servings

1 package Duncan Hines
  Deluxe Fudge Marble
  Cake Mix
3 large eggs
⅓ cup Crisco Oil or Puritan
  Oil
1¼ cups water
1 cup whipping cream
1 cup milk
1 package (4-serving-size)
  chocolate instant pudding
  and pie filling mix

1. Preheat oven to 350°F. Grease and flour two 8×1½- or 9×1½-inch round layer pans.

2. Combine dry cake mix, eggs, oil and water in large mixer bowl. Mix as directed on package but do not add contents of small packet. Turn half of batter (about 2½ cups) into one pan. Blend contents of small packet into remaining batter and turn into remaining pan.

3. Bake and cool layers as directed on package. Chill cooled layers to make splitting easier. Split each layer into two thin layers.

4. Whip cream until stiff. Blend in milk and pudding mix. Let set 1 minute.

5. Place one chocolate layer on plate. Spread one-fourth pudding mixture over layer. Top with remaining layers, alternating light and dark layers and spreading pudding mixture between layers. Frost top layer with pudding mixture. Refrigerate until ready to serve.

CHOCOLATE CHEESE TORTE

12 servings

1 package Duncan Hines
  Deluxe Devil's Food
  Cake Mix
3 large eggs
½ cup Crisco Oil or
  Puritan Oil
1⅓ cups water
1 package (8 ounces) cream
  cheese, softened
½ cup (1 stick) butter or
  margarine, softened
1 tablespoon unsweetened
  cocoa
1 teaspoon vanilla extract
1 pound confectioners'
  sugar
  Grated chocolate or
  chocolate curls, if desired

1. Preheat oven to 400°F. Grease two 15½×10½×1-inch jelly roll pans. Line with waxed paper and grease paper.

2. Combine dry cake mix, eggs, oil and water in large mixer bowl. Mix cake as directed on package except increase beating time to 10 minutes. Divide batter evenly in pans. (If you have only one jelly roll pan, bake half the batter at a time.)

3. Bake at 400°F for 8 to 10 minutes or until toothpick inserted in centers comes out clean. Immediately invert each pan on foil-covered cookie sheet. Remove pans and peel off waxed paper. Cool on racks. Trim edges; refrigerate at least 1 hour.

4. For frosting, beat cream cheese and butter in mixer bowl until smooth and creamy. Beat in cocoa and vanilla extract. Add confectioners' sugar, beating until smooth and creamy. Spread on both cakes. Cut each cake into 4 pieces and stack. Decorate with grated chocolate or chocolate curls, if desired. Refrigerate until ready to serve. Store leftover cake in refrigerator.

PINEAPPLE BLITZ TORTE

12 to 16 servings

1 package Duncan Hines
  Deluxe Pineapple Cake
  Mix
4 large eggs, separated
⅓ cup Crisco Oil or Puritan
  Oil
1¼ cups water
¾ cup plus 1 tablespoon
  sugar
¼ cup chopped nuts
½ cup whipping cream
½ teaspoon vanilla extract
½ cup well-drained crushed
  pineapple

1. Preheat oven to 350°F. Grease and flour two 9×1½-inch round layer pans.

2. Combine dry cake mix, egg yolks, oil and water in large mixer bowl. Mix cake as directed on package. Divide batter evenly in pans.

3. Beat egg whites until frothy. Gradually add ¾ cup sugar, beating until stiff peaks form. Carefully spread meringue over batter. Sprinkle with nuts.

4. Bake at 350°F for 30 to 35 minutes. Cool in pans on racks 15 minutes; remove layers from pans and cool completely, meringue-side-up, on racks.

5. For filling, beat cream until stiff; beat in 1 tablespoon sugar and vanilla extract. Fold in crushed pineapple.

6. Place one cake layer, meringue-side-down, on plate; spread with filling. Place second layer, meringue-side-up, on top. Refrigerate.

*Open House Ribbon Torte (top),
Pineapple Blitz Torte (bottom)*

ANGEL PECAN FLUFF CAKE

1 package Duncan Hines Deluxe Angel Food Cake Mix
1⅓ cups water
1 envelope unflavored gelatin
1 cup cold milk
2 egg yolks
¾ cup sugar
2 teaspoons vanilla extract
1 cup whipping cream, whipped
¾ cup coarsely chopped pecans
2 tablespoons butter or margarine, melted
½ teaspoon salt

1. Preheat oven to 375°F.

2. Prepare cake with water as directed on package. Pour batter into ungreased 10-inch tube pan. Cut through batter with knife or spatula to remove large air bubbles.

3. Bake at 375°F for 30 to 40 minutes or until top crust is golden brown, firm and dry. Do not underbake. To cool, hang upside down on funnel or bottle at least 1½ hours.

4. For frosting, sprinkle gelatin over milk in small saucepan. Let stand 1 minute to soften. Heat just to boiling over low heat, stirring until gelatin is dissolved. Beat egg yolks in bowl until light. Add hot milk mixture while stirring vigorously. Add sugar and vanilla extract; stir until sugar is dissolved. Refrigerate until almost set, stirring occasionally. Fold in whipped cream. Refrigerate until frosting is of spreading consistency. Spread over cake.

5. Combine pecans, butter and salt; sprinkle over frosted cake. Refrigerate until ready to serve. Store leftover cake in refrigerator.

STRAWBERRIES ROMANOFF ON ANGEL SLICES

12 to 16 servings

1 package Duncan Hines Deluxe Angel Food Cake Mix
1⅓ cups water
1½ pints fresh strawberries, hulled and halved lengthwise
⅓ cup orange juice
3 tablespoons orange-flavored liqueur
2 tablespoons sugar
1 cup whipping cream
½ teaspoon vanilla extract

1. Preheat oven to 375°F.

2. Prepare cake with water as directed on package. Pour batter into ungreased 10-inch tube pan. Cut through batter with knife or spatula to remove large air bubbles.

3. Bake at 375°F for 30 to 40 minutes or until top crust is golden brown, firm and dry. Do not underbake. To cool, hang pan upside down on funnel or bottle at least 1½ hours.

4. Place strawberries in bowl. Combine orange juice, 2 tablespoons of the liqueur and sugar; pour over strawberries. Cover with plastic wrap. Refrigerate, occasionally spooning liquid over strawberries.

5. Beat whipping cream until soft peaks form. Beat in remaining 1 tablespoon liqueur and vanilla extract. Beat until thick. Refrigerate until ready to use.

6. To serve, cut cake into slices. Spoon some strawberries and liquid over cake slices; top with whipped cream.

ELEGANT ANGEL TORTE

12 to 16 servings

1 package Duncan Hines
   Deluxe Angel Food Cake
   Mix
1⅓ cups water
2 cups whipping cream
¼ cup chocolate syrup
1 tablespoon sugar
⅓ cup orange marmalade
6 red maraschino cherries
   with stems, if desired
6 pecan halves, if desired
¼ cup chocolate curls, if
   desired

1. Preheat oven to 375°F.

2. Prepare cake with water as directed on package. Pour batter into ungreased 10-inch tube pan. Cut through batter with knife or spatula to remove large air bubbles.

3. Bake at 375°F for 30 to 40 minutes or until top crust is golden brown, firm and dry. Do not underbake. To cool, hang pan upside down on funnel or bottle at least 1½ hours.

4. Slice cooled cake crosswise into four 1-inch layers.

5. Whip cream until stiff. Beat in chocolate syrup and sugar. Place bottom cake slice on serving plate; spread with ⅓ cup whipped cream. Top with next layer; spread with orange marmalade. Top with next layer; spread with ⅓ cup whipped cream. Add final layer. Frost sides and top with remaining whipped cream. Decorate with cherries, pecans and chocolate curls.

CHOCOLAT AU RHUM

12 to 16 servings

1 package Duncan Hines
   Deluxe Devil's Food Cake
   Mix
4 large eggs
½ cup Crisco Oil or Puritan
   Oil
1¼ cups water
1 package (4-serving-size)
   chocolate instant pudding
   and pie filling mix
¾ cup light corn syrup
¾ cup light rum or ¾ cup
   water plus ½ to ¾
   teaspoon rum extract
1 cup whipping cream
2 tablespoons sugar
½ teaspoon vanilla extract
   Grated chocolate, if
   desired

1. Preheat oven to 350°F. Grease and flour 10-inch tube pan.

2. Combine dry cake mix, eggs, oil, water and pudding mix in large mixer bowl. Mix cake as directed on package. Turn batter into pan and spread evenly.

3. Bake at 350°F for 50 to 60 minutes. Cool in pan 15 minutes.

4. Blend corn syrup and rum. Slowly pour half of syrup over top of warm cake in pan. Let cake cool completely, then remove from pan; turn upside down on serving platter and pour remaining syrup over cake. Let stand several hours.

5. To serve, beat cream until stiff; beat in sugar and vanilla extract. Slice cake and top with whipped cream. Sprinkle grated chocolate over whipped cream.

GLAZED APRICOT LAYER

8 servings

1 package Duncan Hines
   Deluxe Yellow Cake Mix
3 large eggs
⅓ cup Crisco Oil or Puritan
   Oil
1¼ cups water
¾ cup flaked coconut
1 can (16 ounces) apricot
   halves in syrup
½ cup apricot preserves

1. Preheat oven to 350°F. Grease and flour two 9×1½-inch pans.

2. Combine dry cake mix, eggs, oil and water in large mixer bowl. Mix cake as directed on package. Divide batter evenly in pans. Sprinkle coconut over batter in one pan. Bake and cool as directed on package.

3. Place cooled coconut cake layer on plate. (Wrap and freeze plain layer for another use.)

4. Drain apricots, reserving 1 tablespoon syrup. Arrange apricot halves cut-side-down around edge of cake. Combine apricot preserves and 1 tablespoon reserved syrup in small saucepan. Heat, stirring occasionally, over low heat until the mixture is warm. Spoon mixture over each apricot, allowing it to drizzle down sides of cake. Refrigerate until ready to serve.

Elegant Angel Torte (top),
Glazed Apricot Layer (bottom)

KAHLUA CHOCOLATE CAKE

12 to 16 servings

*1 package Duncan Hines
    Deluxe Swiss Chocolate
    Cake Mix*
⅔ cup water
⅓ cup Kahlua
3 large eggs
*⅓ cup Crisco Oil or
    Puritan Oil*
*1 envelope (1¼ ounces)
    whipped topping mix*
*1 package (4-serving-size)
    pistachio instant pudding
    and pie filling mix*
1½ cups cold milk

1. Preheat oven to 350°F. Grease and flour two 9×1½-inch round layer pans.

2. Combine dry cake mix, water, Kahlua, eggs and oil in large mixer bowl. Mix cake as directed on package. Divide batter evenly in pans.

3. Bake at 350°F for 30 to 35 minutes or until toothpick inserted in centers comes out clean. Cool in pans on wire racks 10 minutes. Remove from pans; cool completely on racks.

4. For frosting, blend topping mix, instant pudding mix and cold milk in chilled deep bowl. Beat with chilled beaters until stiff (3 to 8 minutes). Spread between cooled layers and on sides and top of cake. Refrigerate until ready to serve. Store leftover cake in refrigerator.

COFFEE CREAM ANGEL CAKE

12 to 14 servings

*1 package Duncan Hines
    Deluxe Angel Food Cake
    Mix*
1⅓ cups water
*1 package (4-serving-size)
    vanilla pudding and pie
    filling mix*
1½ cups milk
*1 tablespoon powdered
    instant coffee*
2 cups whipping cream
¼ cup sugar
1 teaspoon vanilla extract
¼ cup chopped nuts

1. Preheat oven to 375°F.

2. Prepare cake with water as directed on package. Pour batter into ungreased 10-inch tube pan. Cut through batter with knife or spatula to remove large air bubbles.

3. Bake at 375°F for 30 to 40 minutes or until top crust is golden brown, firm and looks dry. Do not underbake. To cool, hang pan upside down on funnel or bottle at least 1½ hours.

4. Combine pudding mix, milk and coffee powder in saucepan. Cook pudding as directed on package. Cool to room temperature.

5. Place cake, wider-side-down, on serving plate. Cut around cake 1½ inches from outer edge and 2 inches down into cake. Gently remove center; tear into small pieces. Tightly fill the bottom of the hole with some of the cake pieces. Reserve remaining pieces.

6. Whip cream until stiff; beat in sugar and vanilla extract. Beat pudding smooth; fold two-thirds whipped cream and remaining cake pieces into pudding. Turn coffee cream mixture into cake shell. Sprinkle filling with nuts. Spread remaining whipped cream on sides and top edge of cake. Refrigerate until firm, preferably overnight.

Coffee Cream Angel Cake

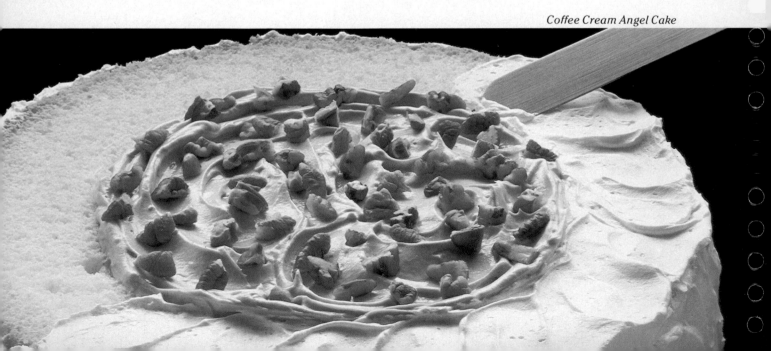

APRICOT SUPREME CAKE

12 to 16 servings

1 package Duncan Hines Deluxe White Cake Mix
1 cup plus 3 tablespoons apricot nectar
4 large eggs
½ cup Crisco Oil or Puritan Oil
1 package (4-serving-size) vanilla instant pudding and pie filling mix
6 tablespoons butter or margarine
½ teaspoon vanilla extract
4 cups confectioners' sugar
1 can (8¾ ounces) apricot halves, drained
Mint leaves, if desired

1. Preheat oven to 350°F. Grease and flour 10-inch tube pan.

2. Combine dry cake mix, 1 cup apricot nectar, eggs, oil and pudding mix in large mixer bowl. Beat 4 minutes at medium speed. Turn batter into pan and spread evenly.

3. Bake at 350°F for 50 to 55 minutes or until toothpick inserted in center comes out clean. Cool in pan on rack 10 minutes. Remove from pan. Cool completely on rack.

4. For frosting, cream butter and vanilla extract in bowl. Add confectioners' sugar alternately with remaining 3 tablespoons apricot nectar, beating until smooth after each addition. Spread on cooled cake and decorate with apricot halves and mint leaves.

ORANGE SUPREME CAKE

12 to 16 servings

1 package Duncan Hines
Deluxe Lemon Cake Mix
1 tablespoon grated coconut
2 tablespoons grated orange
peel, divided
1 cup undiluted evaporated
milk
⅓ cup plus ¾ cup orange
juice, divided
6 large eggs
⅓ cup Crisco Oil or
Puritan Oil
¾ cup sugar
1 cup whipping cream
¼ teaspoon almond extract
¼ teaspoon vanilla extract
*Toasted almonds, if
desired
Mandarin orange
segments, if desired*

1. Preheat oven to 350°F. Grease and flour two 8×1½-inch round layer pans.

2. Combine dry cake mix, coconut, 1 tablespoon orange peel, evaporated milk, ⅓ cup orange juice, 3 eggs and oil in large mixer bowl. Mix cake as directed on package. Divide batter evenly in pans.

3. Bake at 350°F for 30 to 35 minutes or until toothpick inserted in centers comes out clean. Cool in pans on racks 10 minutes. Remove from pans; cool completely on racks. Refrigerate cooled layers for ease in splitting.

4. For orange filling, beat 3 eggs until blended in small saucepan. Stir in sugar, ¾ cup orange juice and 1 tablespoon orange peel. Cook and stir over low heat until thick, about 10 minutes. Cool.

5. Whip cream until stiff. Fold whipped cream, almond extract and vanilla extract into egg mixture.

6. Split each layer into two thin layers. Spread filling between layers and on top of cake. Decorate with toasted almonds and mandarin orange segments, if desired. Refrigerate until ready to serve. Store leftover cake in refrigerator.

RUM-SAUCED CAKE WEDGES

16 servings

1 package Duncan Hines
*Butter Recipe Fudge
Cake Mix*
3 large eggs
½ cup butter or margarine,
softened
⅔ cup water
3 egg yolks
½ cup sugar
3 tablespoons water
1 cup whipping cream
2 tablespoons rum or
⅛ teaspoon rum extract
½ teaspoon vanilla extract

1. Preheat oven to 375°F. Grease and flour two 9×1½-inch round layer pans.

2. Combine dry cake mix, 3 whole eggs, butter and ⅔ cup water in large mixer bowl. Mix, bake and cool cake as directed on package.

3. For sauce, beat 3 egg yolks in small mixer bowl with electric mixer at high speed 3 minutes. Combine sugar and 3 tablespoons water in small saucepan. Cook and stir over medium heat until sugar is dissolved. Continue cooking without stirring until temperature reaches 240° on candy thermometer. Slowly pour hot syrup into egg yolks while beating at high speed. Beat until mixture is very thick. Refrigerate for about 20 minutes.

4. Whip cream until stiff; fold in cooled egg mixture. Fold in rum and vanilla extract. Cut layers into wedges and serve with sauce.

ICE CREAM TORTE

15 servings

1 package Duncan Hines
*Deluxe Deep Chocolate
Cake Mix*
3 large eggs
½ cup Crisco Oil or
Puritan Oil
1¼ cups water
½ gallon brick vanilla ice
cream
1 cup whipping cream
2 tablespoons sugar
1 teaspoon vanilla extract
*Chocolate jimmies, if
desired*

1. Preheat oven to 350°F. Line two 15½×10½×1-inch jelly roll pans with waxed paper. (If you have only one jelly roll pan, bake half the batter at a time.)

2. Combine dry cake mix, eggs, oil and water in large mixer bowl. Mix cake as directed on package. Divide batter evenly in pans.

3. Bake at 350°F for 15 to 20 minutes or until toothpick inserted in centers comes out clean. Immediately invert onto towel. Peel off waxed paper. Cool on racks.

4. Slice cooled cakes in half lengthwise. Slice ice cream lengthwise into six 6½×4½×⅔-inch slices. Starting with cake alternate one cake slice with two slices of ice cream laid end to end.

5. Whip cream in chilled bowl until stiff. Beat in sugar and vanilla extract. Frost top of torte with whipped cream and sprinkle with chocolate jimmies, if desired. Freeze until ready to serve.

*Orange Supreme Cake (top),
Ice Cream Torte (bottom)*

ANGEL FOOD À LA FLAMBÉ

12 servings

1 package Duncan Hines
   Deluxe Angel Food
   Cake Mix
1⅓ cups water
6 canned apricot halves
1 cup strawberry preserves
¼ cup plus 2 tablespoons rum

1. Preheat oven to 375°F.

2. Prepare cake with water as directed on package. Pour batter into ungreased 10-inch tube pan. Cut through batter with knife or spatula to remove large air bubbles.

3. Bake at 375°F for 30 to 40 minutes or until top crust is golden brown, firm and dry. Do not underbake. To cool, hang pan upside down on funnel or bottle at least 1½ hours.

4. Arrange apricot halves on top of cooled cake.

5. Combine strawberry preserves and 2 tablespoons rum in small saucepan. Heat until warm. Glaze cake and apricots with warm mixture. Heat ¼ cup rum in small saucepan, then ignite with match and spoon over cake.

VIENNESE CHERRY CHEESE TORTE

12 to 16 servings

1 package Duncan Hines
   Butter Recipe Golden
   Cake Mix
3 large eggs
½ cup (1 stick) butter or
   margarine, softened
⅔ cup water
1 package (8 ounces) plus 1
   package (3 ounces) cream
   cheese, softened
⅔ cup sugar
¼ teaspoon ground nutmeg
2 tablespoons milk
1 can (21 ounces) cherry pie
   filling

1. Preheat oven to 375°F. Grease and flour two 8×1½- or 9×1½-inch round layer pans.

2. Combine dry cake mix, eggs, butter and water in large mixer bowl. Mix, bake and cool as directed on package. Refrigerate layers to make splitting easier. Split each cake into 2 thin layers.

3. For filling, beat cream cheese, sugar, nutmeg and milk until smooth.

4. Place one layer on cake plate. Spread with ½ cup cream cheese filling; top with ½ cup cherry filling. Repeat layers, ending with cake layer. Spread remaining cream cheese filling over top layer and top with remaining cherry filling. Refrigerate until ready to serve.

STRAWBERRY PARFAIT CAKE

16 servings

1 package Duncan Hines
   Deluxe White Cake Mix
3 egg whites or 3 whole eggs
⅓ cup Crisco Oil or
   Puritan Oil
1¼ cups water
   Few drops green food
   coloring
   Few drops red food
   coloring
⅔ cup light corn syrup
1 egg white
⅛ teaspoon salt
½ vanilla extract
1 package (10 ounces)
   frozen strawberries,
   thawed
1 tablespoon cornstarch

1. Preheat oven to 350°F. Grease and flour two 8×1½-inch round layer pans.

2. Combine dry cake mix, 3 egg whites or 3 whole eggs, oil and water in large mixer bowl. Mix cake as directed on package. Divide batter in half. Add green coloring to one half to tint pale green; turn into one pan. Tint remaining batter pink with red food coloring and turn into remaining pan.

3. Bake and cool as directed on package.

4. For frosting, heat corn syrup to boiling in small saucepan. Combine 1 egg white, salt and vanilla extract in small bowl. Beat at high speed until stiff, not dry peaks form. Slowly beat in hot syrup; beat 5 to 7 minutes or until frosting holds shape. Spread frosting between layers and on sides and top of cake.

5. For strawberry glaze, drain strawberries, reserving syrup. Blend reserved syrup and cornstarch in small saucepan. Cook over medium heat until mixture boils and thickens. Stir in strawberries. Cool. Pour over top of cake, letting some run down sides. Refrigerate until glaze sets.

Angel Food à la Flambé (top),
Viennese Cherry Cheese Torte (bottom)

CHOCOLATE CHERRY TORTE

9 to 12 servings

1 **package Duncan Hines Deluxe Devil's Food Cake Mix**
3 **large eggs**
½ **cup Crisco Oil or Puritan Oil**
1⅓ **cups water**
1 **can (17.5 ounces) ready-to-serve chocolate pudding**
5 **tablespoons rum**
1 **cup coarsely chopped walnuts**
¾ **cup red maraschino cherries, quartered and drained**
1 **container (4 ounces) frozen non-dairy whipped topping, thawed**
2 **ounces (2 squares) unsweetened chocolate, shaved with paring knife or vegetable peeler**

1. Preheat oven to 350°F. Grease and flour two 9×9×2-inch pans.

2. Combine dry cake mix, eggs, oil and water in large mixer bowl. Mix cake as directed on package. Divide batter evenly in pans.

3. Bake at 350°F for 25 to 30 minutes or until toothpick inserted in center comes out clean. Cool in pans on racks 10 minutes. Remove from pans; cool completely on racks. Chill cooled layers to make splitting easier.

4. For filling, place pudding in bowl. Blend in 1 tablespoon rum, walnuts and cherries. Fold in whipped topping.

5. Split each cake into 2 thin layers. Place one top layer cut-side-down on serving plate and drizzle with 1 tablespoon rum. Spread one-fourth of filling mixture over layer, almost to edges. Sprinkle with one-fourth of chocolate. Place bottom layer on filling; press lightly. Drizzle cake with 1 tablespoon rum. Spread evenly with one-fourth of filling and sprinkle with one-fourth chocolate. Place bottom half of remaining layer on stack and drizzle with 1 table-spoon rum. Top with one-fourth filling and one-fourth chocolate. Place remaining layer on cake, cut-side-down. Drizzle with remaining tablespoon rum; spread with remaining filling and top with remaining chocolate. Refrigerate until set.

PETITS FOURS

70 cakes

1 **package Duncan Hines Deluxe Cherry, White or Yellow Cake Mix**
3 **large eggs**
⅓ **cup Crisco Oil or Puritan Oil**
1¼ **cups water**
3 **cups granulated sugar**
¼ **teaspoon cream of tartar**
1½ **cups hot water**
1 **teaspoon vanilla extract**
2¼ **cups confectioners' sugar**
   Food coloring, if desired
   Frosted Roses or candy decorations, if desired

1. Preheat oven to 350°F. Line 15½×10½×1-inch jelly roll pan with waxed paper.

2. Combine dry cake mix, eggs, oil and 1¼ cups water in large mixer bowl. Mix cake as directed on package. Turn batter into pan and spread evenly.

3. Bake at 350°F for 25 to 30 minutes or until toothpick inserted in center comes out clean. Immediately turn cake out onto towel and peel off paper. Cool.

4. Cut cooled cake into seventy 1½-inch shapes. Place on racks with waxed paper under racks.

5. For frosting, combine granulated sugar, cream of tartar, and 1½ cups hot water in heavy saucepan. Cook over medium heat until syrup reaches 226°F on candy thermometer. Cool until lukewarm (110°F). Stir in vanilla extract. Gradually beat in confectioners' sugar until frosting is of good pouring consistency. Tint frosting with food coloring, if desired.

6. Pour frosting over cakes on racks. After frosting one rack, remove frosting from waxed paper and return to bowl of frosting. If frosting becomes too thick, heat over hot water or add a few drops of hot water. Repeat until all cakes are frosted. Decorate with frosted roses or candy decorations.

Chocolate Cherry Torte (top),
Petits Fours (bottom)

Children's Party Cakes

MISTER FUNNY FACE

24 servings

1 package Duncan Hines Deluxe White Cake Mix
3 large egg whites or 3 large whole eggs
⅓ cup Crisco Oil or Puritan Oil
1¼ cups water
½ gallon vanilla ice cream
Whole pecans
Dark raisins
Red hots
1 quart fresh strawberries, halved or 2 packages (10 ounces each) frozen strawberry halves, thawed

1. Preheat oven to 350°F. Line 24 muffin cups with paper baking cups or grease and flour muffin cups.

2. Combine dry cake mix, egg whites, oil and water in large mixer bowl. Mix cake as directed on package. Spoon batter into muffin cups, filling half full.

3. Bake at 350°F for 15 to 20 minutes or until toothpick inserted in center comes out clean. Cool for 15 minutes. (Remove liners if used.)

4. To serve, turn each cupcake upside down on dessert plate. Place one scoop ice cream on top. Decorate ice cream as face, using whole pecans for ears, raisins for eyes and red hots for mouth. Spoon strawberries around bottom of cupcake; place one strawberry half on top as hat.

CHILDREN'S DELIGHT

24 servings

1 package Duncan Hines Deluxe Chocolate Chip Cake Mix
½ cup graham cracker crumbs
3 large eggs
⅓ cup Crisco Oil or Puritan Oil
1¼ cups water
12 large marshmallows, cut in half
1 package (6 ounces) semisweet chocolate pieces
4 tablespoons butter or margarine
2 tablespoons corn syrup

1. Preheat oven to 350°F. Grease and flour 13×9×2-inch pan.

2. Combine dry cake mix and graham cracker crumbs in large mixer bowl. Add eggs, oil and water; blend on low speed, then beat 2 minutes on high speed. Turn batter into pan and spread evenly.

3. Bake at 350°F for 30 to 35 minutes or until toothpick inserted in center comes out clean.

4. Place marshmallow halves on warm cake. Cool cake in pan on rack.

5. Melt chocolate pieces with butter and corn syrup in small saucepan; drizzle over marshmallows and cake.

Mister Funny Face

CLOWN PARTY CAKE

12 to 16 servings

1 package Duncan Hines Deluxe Cake Mix (any flavor)
3 large eggs
   Crisco Oil or Puritan Oil
   Water
5 cups confectioners' sugar
¾ cup Crisco shortening
⅓ cup non-dairy creamer
2 teaspoons vanilla extract
½ cup water
½ teaspoon salt
   Red food coloring
   Yellow food coloring
   Assorted candies

1. Preheat oven to 350°F. Grease and flour one 8×1½-inch round layer pan and one 8×8×2-inch pan.

2. Combine dry cake mix, eggs, and the amount of oil and water listed on package in large mixer bowl. Mix cake as directed on package. Turn about 2 cups batter into round pan and about 3 cups batter into square pan; spread evenly. Batter should be about ¾-inch deep.

3. Bake at 350°F for 30 to 35 minutes or until toothpick inserted in center comes out clean. Cool in pans on racks 10 minutes. Remove from pans; cool completely on racks.

4. For decorator frosting, beat confectioners' sugar, shortening, non-dairy creamer, vanilla extract, ½ cup water and salt in large mixer bowl 3 minutes at medium speed, then for 5 minutes at high speed. Add more confectioners' sugar to thicken or more water to thin frosting as needed. Measure 1½ cups frosting and color with red food coloring. Measure 1 cup frosting and color with yellow food coloring.

5. Cut cooled cake and arrange as shown. Spread white frosting on round layer and red frosting on hat and bow tie. Decorate with assorted candies and white frosting. Make zigzag border using decorator bag with star tip. Use candies for face. Make yellow hair using decorator bag and star tip.

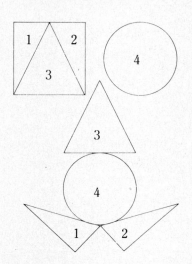

BIRTHDAY CAKELETS

24 servings

2 packages Duncan Hines Deluxe Devil's Food Cake Mix
6 large eggs
1 cup Crisco Oil or Puritan Oil
2⅔ cups water
2 cups light corn syrup
4 large egg whites
⅛ teaspoon salt
   Red food coloring
½ teaspoon peppermint extract

1. Preheat oven to 350°F. Grease and flour two 13×9×2-inch pans.

2. Combine dry cake mix, whole eggs, oil and water in large mixer bowl. Mix, bake and cool cakes as directed on package. Freeze cooled cakes at least 2 hours.

3. For frosting, heat syrup to boiling. Beat egg whites in large mixer bowl at medium speed until frothy. Add salt and continue beating until soft peaks form. Turn mixer to high speed and gradually add hot corn syrup, beating until soft peaks form. Fold in food coloring to tint delicate pink. Fold in peppermint extract.

4. Draw heart on 3-inch square of cardboard; cut out. Set heart pattern on lower left corner of one cake. Cut around pattern through cake. Cut out 11 more hearts before removing cake pieces. Repeat with remaining cake.

5. Frost sides and tops of each cake heart. Insert pink birthday candle in center of each heart.

Clown Party Cake (top),
Birthday Cakelets (bottom)

ICE CREAM CONE CAKES

12 to 16 servings

1 package Duncan Hines Deluxe Cake Mix (any flavor)
3 large eggs
Crisco Oil or Puritan Oil
Water
1 package (6 ounces) semisweet chocolate pieces
5 cups confectioners' sugar
¾ cup Crisco shortening
⅓ cup non-dairy creamer
½ cup water
2 teaspoons vanilla extract
Chocolate jimmies
Red maraschino cherries with stems

1. Preheat oven to 350°F. Grease and flour one 8×1½-inch round layer pan and one 8×8×2-inch pan.

2. Combine dry cake mix, eggs and the amount of oil and water listed on package in large mixer bowl. Mix cake as directed on package. Turn about 2 cups batter into round pan and about 3 cups batter into square pan; spread evenly. (Batter should be ¾-inch deep.)

3. Bake at 350°F for 30 to 35 minutes or until toothpick inserted in center comes out clean. Cool in pans on racks 10 minutes. Remove from pans; cool completely on racks.

4. For frosting, melt chocolate in saucepan over low heat; set aside. Combine confectioners' sugar, shortening, non-dairy creamer, water and vanilla in large mixer bowl. Beat at medium speed 3 minutes, then at high speed 5 minutes. Add more confectioners' sugar to thicken or more water to thin frosting as needed. Divide frosting in half. Blend melted chocolate into one half.

5. Cut cooled cake and arrange as shown. Spread some of the chocolate frosting on cone parts. Decorate with remaining chocolate frosting, using decorator bag and writing tip (see photo). Spread white frosting on ice cream part of cake. Sprinkle chocolate jimmies over cones and decorate ice cream part with cherries.

  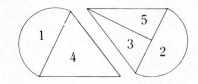

JELLY BEAN CIRCUS CAKE

14 servings

1 package Duncan Hines Deluxe Lemon Cake Mix
3 large eggs
⅓ cup Crisco Oil or Puritan Oil
1¼ cups water
½ cup (1 stick) butter or margarine
1 teaspoon vanilla extract
3 egg yolks
3 cups confectioners' sugar
4 ounces (4 squares) semisweet chocolate, melted
¼ cup half-and-half
14 small animal crackers
1 six-inch colored candy stick
70 jelly beans

1. Preheat oven to 350°F. Grease and flour two 9×1½-inch round layer pans.

2. Combine dry cake mix, whole eggs, oil and water in large mixer bowl. Mix, bake and cool cake as directed on package.

3. For frosting*, cream butter, vanilla extract and egg yolks in small bowl. Gradually add confectioners' sugar, beating after each addition. Beat in melted chocolate and half-and-half. Beat 3 to 5 minutes or until frosting is of spreading consistency. Spread between cooled layers and on sides and top of cake.

4. Press animal crackers around bottom edge of cake. Place candy stick in center, and if desired attach paper pennant. Arrange jelly beans in spoke fashion, from candy stick to edge of cake.

*Or use 1 can Duncan Hines Dark Dutch Fudge or Chocolate Frosting.

Ice Cream Cone Cakes

CHOCOLATE BUTTERSCOTCH CHIP CUPCAKES

24 cupcakes

½ cup cake flour
1 package (6 ounces) butterscotch-flavored pieces (1 cup), divided
1 package (6 ounces) semisweet chocolate pieces (1 cup), divided
1 package Duncan Hines Deluxe White Cake Mix
3 egg whites or 3 whole eggs
⅓ cup Crisco Oil or Puritan Oil
1¼ cups water

1. Preheat oven to 350°F. Line 24 muffin cups with paper baking cups.

2. Combine cake flour, ½ cup butterscotch pieces and ½ cup chocolate pieces in small bowl.

3. Combine dry cake mix, egg whites or whole eggs, oil and water in large mixer bowl. Mix cake as directed on package. Stir in chocolate-butterscotch mixture. Spoon batter into muffin cups, filling about two-thirds full.

4. Bake at 350°F for 18 to 23 minutes or until toothpick inserted in centers comes out clean. Cool in pans on racks 10 minutes. Remove from pans; cool completely on racks.

5. For chocolate-butterscotch frosting, melt ½ cup butterscotch and ½ cup chocolate pieces in small saucepan over low heat; stir until smooth. Spread over cooled cupcakes.

PUSSYCAT CAKE

12 to 16 servings

1 package Duncan Hines Deluxe Cake Mix (any flavor)
3 large eggs
  Crisco Oil or Puritan Oil
  Water
3¾ cups confectioners' sugar
½ cup Crisco shortening
3 tablespoons non-dairy creamer
1 teaspoon vanilla extract
6 tablespoons water
¼ teaspoon salt
  Assorted candies
  Licorice strings

1. Preheat oven to 350°F. Grease and flour 13×9×2-inch pan.

2. Combine dry cake mix, eggs and the amount of oil and water listed on package in large mixer bowl. Mix, bake and cool cake as directed on package.

3. For frosting, beat confectioners' sugar, shortening, non-dairy creamer, vanilla extract, 6 tablespoons water and salt in large mixer bowl for 2 minutes at medium speed. Then beat 3 minutes at high speed. Add more confectioners' sugar to thicken or water to thin frosting as needed.

4. Cut cooled cake and arrange as shown. Spread frosting on sides and top of cake. Use assorted candies and licorice for face and whiskers.

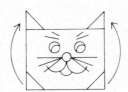

BIG SANDWICH CAKE

10 to 12 servings

1 package Duncan Hines Deluxe Yellow Cake Mix
3 large eggs
⅓ cup Crisco Oil or Puritan Oil
1¼ cups water
1 cup Jif Peanut Butter
1 tablespoon milk
¾ cup grape jelly

1. Preheat oven to 350°F. Grease and flour two 8×8×2-inch pans.

2. Combine dry cake mix, eggs, oil and water in large mixer bowl. Mix batter as directed on package.

3. Bake at 350°F for 35 to 40 minutes or until toothpick inserted in centers comes out clean. Cool cakes in pans on racks 10 minutes. Remove from pans; cool completely on racks.

4. Mix together peanut butter and milk until well blended. Spread evenly over one cooled layer. Stir grape jelly to soften. Spread evenly over peanut butter. Top with second cake layer.

TEDDY BEAR CAKE

12 to 16 servings

1 **package Duncan Hines**
Deluxe Cake Mix (any
flavor)
3 **large eggs**
Crisco Oil or Puritan Oil
Water
1 **can (16 ounces) chocolate**
syrup
1⅓ **cups Jif Creamy Peanut**
Butter
3 **tablespoons light corn**
syrup
2 **cups confectioners' sugar**
½ **cup Crisco shortening**
2 **tablespoons water**
¼ **teaspoon vanilla extract**
Licorice strings
Gumdrops

1. Preheat oven to 350°F. Grease and flour one 10×2-inch round layer pan and 5 muffin cups.

2. Combine dry cake mix, eggs and the amount of oil and water listed on package in large mixer bowl. Mix as directed on package. Fill muffin cups one-half full with batter; turn remaining batter into round pan and spread evenly.

3. Bake at 350°F for 12 to 15 minutes for cupcakes and 50 to 55 minutes for round cake or until toothpicks inserted in centers come out clean. Cool in pans on racks 10 minutes. Remove from pans; cool completely on racks.

4. For chocolate-peanut frosting, combine chocolate syrup, peanut butter and corn syrup; mix well. For white frosting, combine confectioners' sugar, shortening, water and vanilla extract in bowl; beat until smooth and of spreading consistency.

5. Spread chocolate frosting on cooled round cake and two cupcakes for ears. Position ears at top of cake. Place remaining cupcakes on lower portion for snout (see photo). Spread white frosting on snout and ear and eye areas. Use licorice and gumdrops for face.

BACK-TO-SCHOOL PENCIL CAKE

12 to 16 servings

1 package Duncan Hines Deluxe Cake Mix (any flavor)
3 large eggs
Crisco Oil or Puritan Oil
Water
5 cups sifted confectioners' sugar
¾ cup Crisco shortening
⅓ cup non-dairy creamer
½ cup water
2 teaspoons vanilla extract
½ teaspoon salt
Food coloring (red and yellow)
Chocolate jimmies

1. Preheat oven to 350°F. Grease and flour 13×9×2-inch pan.

2. Combine dry cake mix, eggs and amount of oil and water listed on package in large mixer bowl. Mix, bake and cool cake as directed on package.

3. For frosting, combine confectioners' sugar, shortening, non-dairy creamer, water, vanilla and salt in large mixer bowl. Beat 3 minutes at medium speed. Increase to high speed and beat 5 minutes more. Add more confectioners' sugar to thicken or water to thin frosting as needed. Measure a small amount of frosting and tint pink with red food coloring. Color remaining frosting with yellow food coloring.

4. Cut cooled cake and arrange as shown. Spread pink frosting on cake for eraser at one end and for wood at the other end. Spread yellow frosting over remaining cake. Decorate with chocolate jimmies for pencil tip and eraser band.

HOPSCOTCH CAKE

20 to 24 servings

1 *package Duncan Hines*
   Deluxe Yellow Cake Mix
3 *large eggs*
⅓ *cup Crisco Oil or Puritan*
   Oil
1¼ *cups water*
1 *package (6 ounces)*
   butterscotch-flavored
   pieces (1 cup)
3 *tablespoons butter or*
   margarine
3½ *cups confectioners' sugar*
4-5 *tablespoons milk*
8 *licorice sticks*

1. Preheat oven to 350°F. Grease and flour 13×9×2-inch baking pan.

2. Combine dry cake mix, eggs, oil and water in large mixer bowl. Mix, bake and cool cake as directed on package.

3. Combine butterscotch pieces and butter in small saucepan. Melt over low heat, stirring constantly. Combine butterscotch mixture and confectioners' sugar in bowl. Add milk gradually, beating until mixture is of spreading consistency. Spread on cooled cake. Decorate top with licorice sticks to make hopscotch pattern. Sketch numbers in squares.

DRUM LAYER CAKE

12 to 16 servings

1 *package Duncan Hines*
   Deluxe Cake Mix (any
   flavor)
3 *large eggs*
   Crisco Oil or Puritan Oil
   Water
5 *cups confectioners' sugar*
¾ *cup Crisco shortening*
⅓ *cup non-dairy creamer*
2 *teaspoons vanilla extract*
½ *cup water*
½ *teaspoon salt*
   Licorice twists and strings
2 *lollipops*

1. Preheat oven to 350°F. Grease and flour two 8×1½-inch round layer pans.

2. Combine dry cake mix, eggs and the amount of oil and water listed on package in large mixer bowl. Mix, bake and cool cake as directed on package.

3. For decorator frosting, beat confectioners' sugar, shortening, non-dairy creamer, vanilla extract, ½ cup water and salt in large mixer bowl. Beat 3 minutes at medium speed, then 5 minutes at high speed. Add more confectioners' sugar to thicken or water to thin frosting as needed.

4. Spread frosting between cooled layers and on sides and top of cake. Cut lengths of licorice twists and make pattern around sides of cake (see photo). For top and bottom borders, braid three licorice strings together and place on cake. Place lollipops on top for drumsticks.

Drum Layer Cake

CUPCAKE CONES

24 servings

24 flat-bottom ice cream
    cones
  1 package Duncan Hines
    Deluxe Devil's Food Cake
    Mix
  3 large eggs
  ½ cup Crisco Oil or Puritan
    Oil
1⅓ cups water
    Ice cream

1. Preheat oven to 350°F. Set ice cream cones in muffin pans with small cups.

2. Combine dry cake mix, eggs, oil and water in large mixer bowl. Mix cake as directed on package. Spoon 2 tablespoons batter into each cone.

3. Bake at 350°F for 20 to 25 minutes or until toothpick inserted in center comes out clean. Cool on racks.

4. To serve, top each cone with a scoop of ice cream.

CHOCOLATE PEANUT CAKE

12 to 16 servings

  1 package Duncan Hines
    Deluxe White Cake Mix
  3 egg whites or 3 whole eggs
  ⅓ cup Crisco Oil or
    Puritan Oil
1¼ cups water
2½ cups confectioners' sugar
  ¼ cup unsweetened cocoa
  ⅓ cup butter or margarine,
    softened
  3 tablespoons Jif Peanut
    Butter
  3 tablespoons milk
  1 teaspoon vanilla extract
  2 tablespoons peanut halves

1. Preheat oven to 350°F. Grease and flour two 8×1½- or 9×1½-inch round layer pans.

2. Combine dry cake mix, egg whites or whole eggs, oil and water in large mixer bowl. Mix, bake and cool cake as directed on package.

3. For frosting, sift together confectioners' sugar and cocoa; set aside. Cream butter and peanut butter in small mixer bowl. Add sugar-cocoa mixture alternately with milk, beating until smooth after each addition. Beat in vanilla extract. Spread ½ cup frosting on one cooled layer; top with second layer. Spread remaining frosting on sides and top of cake. Sprinkle peanut halves around top edge of cake.

Cupcake Cones

Fudge & Banana Cupcakes

FUDGE 'N' BANANA CUPCAKES

24 cupcakes

1   package Duncan Hines
    Deluxe Devil's Food Cake
    Mix
3   large eggs
½   cup Crisco Oil or Puritan
    Oil
1⅓ cups water
½   cup (1 stick) butter or
    margarine
2   ounces (2 squares)
    unsweetened chocolate
1   pound confectioners'
    sugar
½   cup half-and-half
1   teaspoon vanilla extract
4   medium bananas
2   tablespoons lemon juice

1. Preheat oven to 350°F. Line 24 muffin cups with paper baking cups.

2. Combine dry cake mix, eggs, oil and water in large mixer bowl. Mix, bake and cool cupcakes as directed on package.

3. For frosting*, melt butter and chocolate in heavy saucepan over low heat. Remove from heat. Add confectioners' sugar alternately with half-and-half, mixing until smooth after each addition. Beat in vanilla extract. Add more confectioners' sugar to thicken or milk to thin as needed.

4. Using small paring knife, remove cone-shaped piece from top center of each cupcake. Dot top of each cone with frosting. Frost top of each cupcake spreading frosting down into cone-shaped hole. Slice bananas and dip in lemon juice. Stand three banana slices in each hole. Set cone-shaped pieces, pointed-side-up, on banana slices.

Or use 1 can Duncan Hines Dark Dutch Fudge or Chocolate Frosting.

TOASTY TOPPED CAKE SLICES

16 to 20 servings

1   package Duncan Hines
    Deluxe Yellow Cake Mix
3   large eggs
⅓   cup Crisco Oil or Puritan
    Oil
1¼ cups water
2   medium bananas
2   cups miniature
    marshmallows
1   package (6 ounces)
    semisweet chocolate
    pieces (1 cup)

1. Preheat oven to 350°F. Grease and flour two 8½ × 4½ × 2½-inch loaf pans.

2. Combine dry cake mix, eggs, oil and water in large mixer bowl. Mix cake as directed on package. Divide batter evenly in pans.

3. Bake at 350°F for 40 to 45 minutes or until toothpick inserted in center comes out clean. Cool in pans on racks 10 minutes. Remove from pans; cool completely on racks.

4. Slice each loaf into 8 to 10 slices. Place, cut-side-down, on large baking sheet. Peel and slice bananas; arrange on cake slices. Top with marshmallows and chocolate pieces. Place in 350°F oven 12 to 15 minutes or until chocolate melts.

Note: Slices may be wrapped in foil and heated over campfire instead of in oven.

Holiday Baking

PINEAPPLE CHRISTMAS TREE CAKE

12 to 16 servings

½ cup (1 stick) butter or margarine, melted
1 cup packed brown sugar
1 can (20 ounces) pineapple chunks, drained
Red and green maraschino cherries (about 5 each), cut into quarters
1 package Duncan Hines Deluxe Pineapple Cake Mix
3 large eggs
⅓ cup Crisco Oil or Puritan Oil
1¼ cups water
Sweetened whipped cream, if desired

1. Preheat oven to 350°F.

2. Place melted butter in 13×9×2-inch baking pan. Sprinkle brown sugar evenly in pan. Arrange pineapple chunks in pan to form Christmas tree. Start with one chunk in first row, 2 in second, etc. (see photo). Use 4 chunks to make trunk. Place cherry quarters between pineapple chunks to decorate tree.

3. Combine dry cake mix, eggs, oil and water in large mixer bowl. Mix cake as directed on package. Pour batter over fruit in pan and spread evenly.

4. Bake at 350°F for 48 to 53 minutes or until toothpick inserted in center comes out clean. Let stand 5 minutes; turn upside down onto large platter or cookie sheet. If desired, cut cake around pineapple to form cutout tree. Serve warm with sweetened whipped cream.

DELLA ROBBIA CAKE

12 to 16 servings

1 package Duncan Hines Deluxe Angel Food Cake Mix
1⅓ cups water
1½ teaspoons grated lemon peel
6 tablespoons sugar
1½ tablespoons cornstarch
1 cup water
½ teaspoon vanilla extract
1 tablespoon lemon juice
Few drops red food coloring
6 canned peach slices
6 medium strawberries

1. Preheat oven to 375°F.

2. Prepare cake with 1⅓ cups water as directed on package except add lemon peel along with cake flour mixture (red packet B). Pour batter into 10-inch ungreased tube pan. Cut through batter with knife or spatula to remove large air bubbles.

3. Bake at 375°F for 30 to 40 minutes or until top crust is golden brown, firm and dry. Do not underbake. To cool, hang pan upside down on funnel or bottle at least 1½ hours.

4. For glaze, combine sugar, cornstarch and 1 cup water in small saucepan. Cook over medium high heat until mixture comes to a boil and thickens. Remove from heat. Stir in vanilla extract, lemon juice and food coloring.

5. Top cooled cake with fruit, alternating peach slices and strawberries. Pour glaze over fruit and top of cake. Refrigerate at least 1 hour before serving.

Pineapple Christmas Tree Cake   63

THANKSGIVING CRANBERRY COBBLER

16 servings

1   package Duncan Hines
    Deluxe Yellow Cake Mix
½   teaspoon ground
    cinnamon
¼   teaspoon ground nutmeg
1   cup (2 sticks) butter or
    margarine, softened
½   cup chopped nuts
1   can (21 ounces) peach pie
    filling
1   can (16 ounces) whole
    cranberry sauce
    Vanilla ice cream or
    sweetened whipped cream

1. Preheat oven to 350°F.

2. Combine dry cake mix, cinnamon and nutmeg in bowl. Cut in butter with pastry blender or two knives until crumbly. Stir in nuts; set aside.

3. Combine peach pie filling and cranberry sauce in ungreased 13×9×2-inch pan; mix well. Sprinkle crumb mixture over fruit.

4. Bake at 350°F for 45 to 50 minutes or until golden brown. Serve warm with ice cream or whipped cream.

HOLIDAY COFFEE CAKE

12 to 16 servings

1   package Duncan Hines
    Butter Recipe Golden
    Cake Mix
3   large eggs
½   cup (1 stick) butter or
    margarine, softened
⅔   cup water
1½ cups finely chopped
    walnuts
½   cup sugar
1   teaspoon ground
    cinnamon
2   tablespoons butter or
    margarine, melted
1   cup chopped candied
    cherries and pineapple

1. Preheat oven to 375°F. Grease and flour 13×9×2-inch pan.

2. Combine dry cake mix, eggs, ½ cup soft butter and water in large mixer bowl. Mix cake as directed on package. Turn into pan and spread evenly.

3. Bake at 375°F for 15 minutes.

4. While cake is baking, mix together walnuts, sugar, cinnamon and 2 tablespoons melted butter. Distribute fruit over partially baked cake. Sprinkle with nut mixture.

5. Bake 35 minutes more or until toothpick inserted in center comes out clean. Cool slightly; cut into squares. Cool completely in pan on rack.

CANDY CANE CAKE

12 to 16 servings

1   package Duncan Hines
    Deluxe Cake Mix (any
    flavor)
3   large eggs
    Crisco Oil or Puritan Oil
    Water
5   cups confectioners' sugar
¾   cup Crisco shortening
⅓   cup non-dairy creamer
2   teaspoons vanilla extract
½   cup water
½   teaspoon salt
    Red food coloring

1. Preheat oven to 350°F. Grease and flour 13×9×2-inch pan.

2. Combine dry cake mix, eggs and the amount of oil and water listed on package in large mixer bowl. Mix, bake and cool cake as directed on package.

3. For decorator frosting, beat confectioners' sugar, shortening, non-dairy creamer, vanilla extract, ½ cup water and salt in large mixer bowl for 3 minutes at medium speed, then beat 5 minutes at high speed. Add more confectioners' sugar to thicken or water to thin frosting as needed. Reserve 1½ cups frosting. Color remaining frosting with red food coloring.

4. Cut cooled cake and arrange as shown. Spread white frosting on cake. Mark candy cane stripes and fill in with red frosting using decorator bag with star tip.

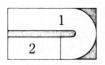   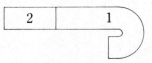

Thanksgiving Cranberry Cobbler (top),
Candy Cane Cake (bottom)

CHRISTMAS FRUIT BARS

About 4 dozen bars

1 package Duncan Hines
   Deluxe Yellow Cake Mix
1 large egg
¼ cup Crisco Oil or Puritan
   Oil
⅓ cup water
1 cup chopped candied
   mixed fruit
½ cup chopped nuts
1 cup confectioners' sugar
2 tablespoons milk
1 teaspoon lemon juice

1. Preheat oven to 375°F. Grease 13×9×2-inch pan.

2. Empty about half of the dry cake mix into bowl. Add egg, oil and water; mix thoroughly by hand or with mixer at low speed. Blend in remaining cake mix (batter will be thick). Stir in candied fruit and nuts. Turn batter into pan and spread evenly.

3. Bake at 375°F for 25 to 30 minutes or until toothpick inserted in center comes out clean. (Bars will appear slightly puffed and will flatten some when removed from oven.) Set pan on rack.

4. For glaze*, mix confectioners' sugar, milk and lemon juice until smooth. Spread over warm layer. Cut into bars.

*Or heat ⅔ cup Duncan Hines Vanilla Frosting in small saucepan over medium heat, stirring constantly, until thin.

HEAVENLY GOLDEN CAKE

12 to 16 servings

1 package Duncan Hines
  Butter Recipe Golden
  Cake Mix
3 large eggs
½ cup (1 stick) butter or
  margarine, softened
⅔ cup water
½ cup packed light brown
  sugar
½ cup chopped walnuts
2 tablespoons milk
2 tablespoons butter or
  margarine
1 cup whipping cream
¼ cup sugar
1 tablespoon grated
  orange peel
1 tablespoon orange juice

1. Preheat oven to 375°F. Grease and flour two 8×1½- or 9×1½-inch round layer pans.

2. Combine dry cake mix, eggs, ½ cup butter and water in large mixer bowl. Mix and bake cake as directed on package. Cool in pans on racks 20 minutes. Remove from pans; set on racks. Place waxed paper under one rack.

3. For filling, combine brown sugar, walnuts, milk and 2 tablespoons butter in small saucepan. Cook and stir over low heat until sugar dissolves. Pour warm topping over one warm layer. Cool completely.

4. For frosting, beat whipping cream in chilled bowl with chilled beaters until stiff. Beat in sugar, orange peel and orange juice. Spread between layers and on sides and top of cake. Serve immediately. Store leftover cake in refrigerator.

GINGERBREAD PEOPLE

About 14 six-inch cookies

1 package Duncan Hines
  Deluxe Spice Cake Mix
2 teaspoons ground ginger
2 large eggs
⅓ cup Crisco Oil or Puritan
  Oil
⅓ cup dark molasses
½ cup all-purpose flour
  Dark raisins

1. Combine all ingredients, except raisins, in large bowl; mix well (mixture will be soft). Refrigerate 2 hours.

2. Preheat oven to 375°F. Roll dough to ¼-inch thickness on lightly floured surface. Cut with 6-inch cookie cutter. Place on ungreased cookie sheets. Press raisins in dough for eyes and buttons.

3. Bake at 375°F for 8 to 10 minutes or until edges just start to brown. Cool several minutes on cookie sheet, then remove to racks to finish cooling.

Gingerbread People

JELLY JEWELS

About 4 dozen 2-inch cookies

1 package Duncan Hines
   Deluxe Yellow Cake Mix
¾ cup Crisco shortening
2 large egg yolks
1 tablespoon milk
2 large egg whites
2 tablespoons water
1¼ cups ground nuts
   Red or green jelly

1. Preheat oven to 375°F. Grease cookie sheets.

2. Combine dry cake mix, shortening, egg yolks and milk; mix well. Shape into 1-inch balls.

3. Combine egg whites and water. Beat with fork until blended. Dip balls in egg white mixture, then roll in nuts. Place 2 inches apart on cookie sheets.

4. Bake at 375°F for 12 to 15 minutes or until golden brown. Immediately press thumb or thimble into center of each cookie making a depression. Cool several minutes on cookie sheets, then remove to racks to finish cooling. Before serving, fill depressions with jelly.

CHOCOLATE FRUIT CAKE

Two 9×5×3-inch loaf cakes

1⅓ cups chopped pitted
   dates
1¼ cups sliced candied
   cherries
1 cup raisins
½ cup chopped candied
   citron
½ cup chopped candied
   pineapple
1 cup chopped walnuts
1 cup chopped pecans
½ cup all-purpose flour
1 package Duncan Hines
   Deluxe Devil's Food
   Cake Mix
⅔ cup water
½ cup sherry
3 large eggs
½ cup Crisco Oil or Puritan
   Oil

1. Preheat oven to 275°F. Grease and flour two 9×5×3-inch loaf pans.

2. Combine fruit, nuts and flour in large bowl; toss until fruit is coated with flour.

3. Combine dry cake mix, water, sherry, eggs and oil in large mixer bowl. Mix cake as directed on package. Stir in fruit and nuts. Turn batter into pans and spread evenly.

4. Bake at 275°F for 3 hours or until toothpick inserted in center comes out clean. Cool in pans 20 minutes. Remove from pans; cool completely on racks.

Note: Cakes may be made 1 week ahead. Wrap tightly in foil.

Chocolate Fruit Cake

COCONUT CRISPS

About 6 dozen 2¼-inch cookies

1 package Duncan Hines
   Deluxe Yellow Cake Mix
½ cup Crisco Oil or Puritan
   Oil
¼ cup water
1 teaspoon almond extract
1 large egg
1 can (3½ ounces) flaked
   coconut
   Whole unblanched
   almonds or red
   maraschino cherries

1. Preheat oven to 350°F.

2. Combine dry cake mix, oil, water, almond extract and egg in bowl; mix well. Stir in coconut. Drop from teaspoon on ungreased baking sheets. Press whole almond or piece of maraschino cherry in center of each cookie.

3. Bake at 350°F for 10 to 12 minutes or until light golden brown. Cool several minutes on cookie sheet, then remove to racks to finish cooling.

LADY BALTIMORE CAKE

12 to 16 servings

1 package Duncan Hines
  Deluxe White Cake Mix
3 egg whites or 3 whole eggs
⅓ cup Crisco Oil or
  Puritan Oil
1¼ cups water
1¼ cups light corn syrup
2 egg whites
¼ teaspoon salt
1 teaspoon vanilla extract
⅓ cup chopped red
  maraschino cherries, well
  drained
⅓ cup chopped raisins
⅓ cup chopped pecans

1. Preheat oven to 350°F. Grease and flour two 8×1½- or 9×1½-inch round layer pans.

2. Combine dry cake mix, 3 egg whites or whole eggs, oil and water in large mixer bowl. Mix, bake and cool cake as directed on package.

3. For frosting, heat corn syrup to boiling. Combine 2 egg whites, salt and vanilla extract in large mixer bowl. Beat at high speed until stiff, not dry peaks form. Slowly pour in hot syrup; beat 5 to 7 minutes or until frosting holds shape.

4. For filling, combine cherries, raisins and pecans with about one-fourth of frosting. Spread between cooled layers. Spread remaining frosting over sides and top of cake. Refrigerate until ready to serve. Decorate with additional raisins, cherries and pecans, if desired.

HOLIDAY FRUIT CAKE

30 to 35 servings

1 pound diced mixed candied fruit
8 ounces candied cherries, chopped
4 ounces candied pineapple, chopped
1½ cups finely chopped nuts
1 cup raisins
½ cup all-purpose flour
1 package Duncan Hines Deluxe Spice Cake Mix
3 large eggs
½ cup Crisco Oil or Puritan Oil
¼ cup water
1 package (4-serving-size) vanilla instant pudding and pie filling mix
Light corn syrup
Candied pineapple slices
Pecan halves

1. Preheat oven to 300°F. Grease one 10-inch tube pan or two 9×5×3-inch loaf pans. Line with heavy paper or aluminum foil.

2. Combine candied fruit, cherries, 4 ounces pineapple, chopped nuts, raisins and flour in bowl; toss until fruit is coated with flour. Set aside.

3. Place dry cake mix, eggs, oil, water and pudding mix in large mixer bowl. Beat 3 minutes at medium speed (batter will be stiff). Stir in candied fruit mixture. Turn batter into pan or pans; spread evenly.

4. Bake at 300°F for 2 hours for tube pan, 1½ hours for loaf pans; cake is done if toothpick inserted in center comes out clean. Cool completely in pans on racks. Remove cake from pans.

5. Heat corn syrup in small saucepan; brush over cake. Decorate with sliced pineapple and pecan halves. To store, wrap in aluminum foil or plastic wrap, or store in airtight container.

YULE LOG

12 to 16 servings

1 package Duncan Hines Deluxe Angel Food Cake Mix
1 cup water
½ cup unsweetened cocoa
¼ cup all-purpose flour
3 large eggs
¾ cup Crisco Oil or Puritan Oil
2½ teaspoons vanilla extract, divided
4¼ cups confectioners' sugar, divided
½ cup orange marmalade
1 tablespoon rum
½ cup (1 stick) butter or margarine, softened, divided
3 tablespoons half-and-half or milk
⅓ cup ground walnuts
2 ounces (2 squares) unsweetened chocolate
4 teaspoons hot water
Walnut halves, if desired

1. Preheat oven to 350°F. Grease and flour 15½×10½×1-inch jelly roll pan and line with waxed paper.

2. Combine egg white mixture (blue "A" packet) and 1 cup water in large mixer bowl. Mix 1 minute at low speed, then beat at high speed until egg whites form very stiff peaks.

3. Sift cocoa, flour and cake flour mixture (red "B" packet) together in bowl. Add eggs, oil and ½ teaspoon vanilla extract; blend, then beat 3 minutes at medium speed. Fold chocolate batter into beaten egg whites. Turn batter into pan to fill to within ¼ inch of top (see Note); spread evenly.

4. Bake at 350°F for 28 to 33 minutes or until toothpick inserted in center comes out clean.

5. Immediately, turn cake onto towel covered with ¼ cup confectioners' sugar. Peel off paper; trim edges of cake. Carefully roll cake with towel from narrow end. Cool on rack.

6. Mix marmalade and rum. Unroll cake and spread marmalade mixture on cake.

7. For filling, beat ¼ cup butter, 1 teaspoon vanilla extract, half-and-half and 3 cups confectioners' sugar in small mixer bowl until fluffy. Stir in ground walnuts. Spread over marmalade. Carefully reroll cake.

8. For glaze, melt chocolate and ¼ cup butter over low heat. Stir in 1 cup confectioners' sugar and 1 teaspoon vanilla extract. Mix in hot water, 1 teaspoon at a time, until glaze is of spreading consistency. Spread over sides and top of cake. Decorate with walnut halves, if desired.

Note: Spoon remaining batter into paper-lined muffin cups, filling about two-thirds full. Bake at 350°F for 15 to 20 minutes. Cool in pans; remove from pans. Frost as desired.

Desserts

PEACH CARROT CHEESECAKE

12 servings

1 package Duncan Hines Deluxe Carrot Cake Mix
½ cup Crisco Oil or Puritan Oil
2 cans (16 ounces each) peach halves in juice
1 envelope unflavored gelatin
2 packages (8 ounces each) cream cheese, softened
1 can (14 ounces) sweetened condensed milk
2 tablespoons lemon juice
1 container (4 ounces) frozen non-dairy whipped topping, thawed
1 teaspoon cornstarch
Mint leaves

1. Preheat oven to 350°F. Grease 10-inch springform pan.

2. For crust, combine dry cake mix and oil in bowl; mix well. Turn into pan and spread evenly. Bake at 350°F for 20 minutes. Cool, then refrigerate.

3. For filling, drain peaches, reserving 1 cup juice. Combine ½ cup of peach juice and gelatin in saucepan. Cook over low heat, stirring constantly until gelatin dissolves. Reserve 3 peach halves for garnish. Purée remaining peaches in blender until smooth. Combine peaches and gelatin mixture; set aside.

4. Beat cream cheese until smooth in large bowl. Add sweetened condensed milk and lemon juice; mix well. Stir in peach gelatin mixture. Fold in whipped topping. Turn into crust-lined pan and spread evenly.

5. To decorate, slice reserved peaches and arrange in 2-piece clusters on top of cheesecake. For glaze, blend remaining ½ cup peach juice and cornstarch in saucepan. Cook and stir until mixture boils and thickens. Cool. Spoon cooled glaze evenly over cheesecake. Add mint leaves to peach clusters. Refrigerate at least 3 hours before serving.

BLUEBERRY CRUNCH

10 to 12 servings

1 can (21 ounces) blueberry pie filling
1 package Duncan Hines Butter Recipe Golden Cake Mix
1 cup packed brown sugar
½ cup (1 stick) butter or margarine, melted
Sweetened whipped cream or ice cream

1. Preheat oven to 350°F.

2. Spread pie filling in bottom of ungreased 9×9×2-inch pan. Mix together dry cake mix, brown sugar and melted butter (mixture will be crumbly). Sprinkle over pie filling.

3. Bake at 350°F for 45 to 55 minutes or until topping is golden brown. Serve warm with sweetened whipped cream or ice cream.

Peach Carrot Cheesecake

HOT FUDGE PUDDING CAKE

16 servings

1 *package Duncan Hines*
  Deluxe Sour Cream
  Chocolate Cake Mix
2 *large eggs*
1 *cup water*
1 *cup chopped pecans*
½ *cup sugar*
½ *cup packed light brown*
  sugar
2 *tablespoons unsweetened*
  cocoa
1 *cup boiling water*
  Sweetened whipped
  cream
  Pecan halves, if desired

1. Preheat oven to 350°F. Grease and flour 13×9×2-inch pan.

2. Combine dry cake mix, eggs and 1 cup water in large mixer bowl. Mix batter as directed on package; stir in chopped pecans. Turn batter into pan and spread evenly. Combine sugar, brown sugar and cocoa. Sprinkle over batter. Pour 1 cup boiling water over all.

3. Bake at 350°F for 45 minutes or until toothpick inserted in center of cake halfway to bottom comes out clean. Serve warm with sweetened whipped cream. Garnish with pecan halves, if desired.

CHOCOLATE REFRIGERATOR DESSERT

12 servings

1 *package Duncan Hines*
  Deluxe Swiss Chocolate
  Cake Mix
3 *large eggs*
½ *cup Crisco Oil or Puritan*
  Oil
1¼ *cups water*
1½ *cups semisweet chocolate*
  pieces
3 *large eggs, separated*
2 *tablespoons sugar*
3 *cups whipped topping*
  Whipped topping for
  garnish
  Red maraschino cherries,
  if desired

1. Preheat oven to 350°F. Grease and flour 10-inch tube pan.

2. Combine dry cake mix, 3 eggs, oil and water in large mixer bowl. Mix, bake and cool cake as directed on package.

3. Melt chocolate in double boiler over hot, not boiling, water. Beat 3 egg yolks with fork. Stir egg yolks and sugar into melted chocolate.

4. Beat 3 egg whites until stiff, not dry, peaks form. Fold beaten egg whites and 3 cups whipped topping into chocolate mixture.

5. Tear cooled cake into small pieces. Place one-third of cake pieces in bottom of 10-inch springform pan. Spoon one-third chocolate mixture over cake pieces. Repeat layers two more times. Refrigerate 24 hours.

6. To serve, unmold and place on serving plate. Decorate with additional whipped topping and garnish with cherries.

Chocolate Refrigerator Dessert

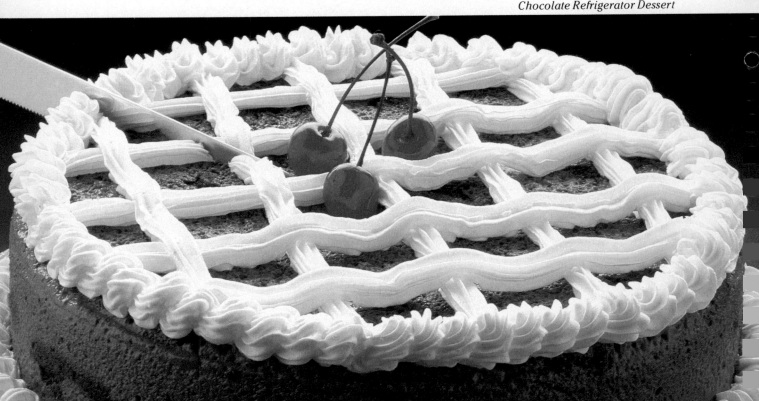

Swedish Apple Cake

SWEDISH APPLE CAKE

16 to 20 servings

1 cup packed brown sugar
2 tablespoons all-purpose flour
¼ teaspoon ground nutmeg
⅛ teaspoon salt
1 cup water
2 tablespoons butter or margarine
1 can (20 ounces) apple pie filling
1 package Duncan Hines Deluxe Lemon Cake Mix
3 large eggs
⅓ cup Crisco Oil or Puritan Oil
1¼ cups water

1. Combine brown sugar, flour, nutmeg and salt in small baking dish. Gradually stir in 1 cup water. Add butter; set aside.

2. Spread apple pie filling in 13×9×2-inch pan.

3. Combine dry cake mix, eggs, oil and 1¼ cups water in large mixer bowl. Mix as directed on package. Spread batter evenly over apples.

4. Place cake and sauce in preheated oven. Bake at 350°F for 43 to 48 minutes or until toothpick inserted in center comes out clean.

5. To serve, spoon warm cake and apples in serving bowls and top with sauce.

GOLDEN CHEESECAKE GEMS

24 servings

1 package Duncan Hines Butter Recipe Golden Cake Mix
¼ cup (½ stick) butter or margarine, melted
2 packages (8 ounces each) cream cheese, softened
3 large eggs
1 cup sugar, divided
1 teaspoon vanilla extract
1½ cups dairy sour cream

1. Preheat oven to 350°F. Grease 24 muffin cups.

2. Combine dry cake mix and melted butter in large mixer bowl. Beat at low speed for 2 minutes (mixture will be crumbly). Divide mixture evenly in muffin cups. Press on bottoms and halfway up sides.

3. Beat cream cheese, eggs, ¾ cup sugar and vanilla extract until smooth. Spoon into muffin cups.

4. Bake at 350°F for 20 minutes or until mixture is set.

5. Combine sour cream and ¼ cup sugar. Spread small amount of topping over each cake. Return to oven for 5 minutes. Cool in pans on racks.

NO-BAKE CHEESECAKE

8 to 12 servings

1 package Duncan Hines
  Deluxe Lemon Cake Mix
¼ teaspoon baking soda
¾ cup plus 2 tablespoons
  Crisco Oil or Puritan Oil
1 package (3 ounces)
  lemon-flavored gelatin
1 cup boiling water
2 packages (8 ounces each)
  cream cheese, softened
1 cup milk

1. Preheat oven to 350°F.

2. Mix together dry cake mix, baking soda and oil. Spread evenly in bottom of ungreased 10-inch springform pan.

3. Bake at 350°F for 25 minutes or until lightly browned. Cool completely.

4. For filling, combine gelatin and boiling water in large mixer bowl; stir to dissolve gelatin. Add cream cheese; beat until smooth. Beat in milk. Pour into cooled crust. Refrigerate until set.

CHERRY CAKE COBBLER

16 servings

1 package Duncan Hines
  Deluxe White Cake Mix
3 large eggs
⅓ cup Crisco Oil or Puritan
  Oil
1¼ cups water
1 cup sugar
2 tablespoons cornstarch
2 cans (16 ounces each)
  pitted red tart cherries
  (undrained)
2 tablespoons butter or
  margarine, melted
1 teaspoon red food coloring
¾ teaspoon almond extract
  Sweetened whipped
  cream or vanilla ice cream

1. Preheat oven to 350°F. Grease and flour 13×9×2-inch pan.

2. Place dry cake mix, eggs, oil and water in large mixer bowl. Mix as directed on package. Turn into pan and spread evenly.

3. Combine sugar and cornstarch in bowl. Add cherries, butter, food coloring and almond extract; mix well. Spoon evenly over batter.

4. Bake at 350°F for 50 to 60 minutes or until golden. Serve warm or cold with whipped cream or ice cream.

Cherry Cake Cobbler

Chocolate Crumb Pie

CHOCOLATE CRUMB PIE

12 to 16 servings

1 package Duncan Hines
  Deluxe Fudge Marble
  Cake Mix
⅔ cup all-purpose flour
½ teaspoon salt
1 large egg
3 tablespoons Crisco Oil or
  Puritan Oil
2 packages (4-serving-size)
  instant or regular
  chocolate pudding and pie
  filling mix
3½ cups milk

1. Preheat oven to 350°F.

2. For crust, combine dry cake mix (do not add contents of small packet), flour, salt, egg and 2 tablespoons oil in large bowl. Mix until crumbs are deeper, even color and uniformly fine (like graham cracker crumbs). Measure 1½ cups of crumb mixture into each of two 9-inch pie plates. Press firmly against sides and then bottom to make crusts; reserve remaining crumb mixture.

3. Prepare pudding mix with milk as directed on package for pie except add half of reserved small packet to each package of pudding mix before mixing or cooking. Pour into crusts. Mix remaining 1 tablespoon oil with reserved crumbs; sprinkle.

4. Bake at 350°F for 20 to 25 minutes or until golden brown. Cool 1 hour, then refrigerate until serving.

DELICIOUS DESSERT SQUARES

16 servings

1 package Duncan Hines
  Deluxe Devil's Food
  Cake Mix
½ cup all-purpose flour
½ teaspoon salt
3 tablespoons Crisco Oil or
  Puritan Oil, divided
1 large egg
2 packages (4-serving-size)
  chocolate instant pudding
  and pie filling mix
4 cups milk

1. Preheat oven to 350°F.

2. Combine dry cake mix, flour and salt in large bowl. Add 2 tablespoons oil and egg. Mix thoroughly with fork or pastry blender until crumbs are uniformly fine. Measure 3 cups crumbs into ungreased 13×9×2-inch pan. Press firmly into bottom and about two-thirds of way up sides of pan.

3. Prepare pudding mix with milk as directed on package and pour into unbaked crust. Add remaining 1 tablespoon oil to remaining crumbs; mix well. Sprinkle over filling.

4. Bake at 350°F for 25 minutes. Cool on rack at room temperature for 1 hour, then refrigerate thoroughly before serving. Store leftover squares in refrigerator.

STRAWBERRY ANGEL DESSERT

20 servings

1   **package Duncan Hines Deluxe Angel Food Cake Mix**
1⅓ **cups water**
1   **can (21 ounces) strawberry pie filling**
1   **package (8 ounces) cream cheese, softened**
¾   **cup milk**
1   **container (8 ounces) frozen non-dairy whipped topping, thawed**

1. Preheat oven to 375°F.

2. Prepare cake mix with water as directed on package. Pour batter into ungreased 10-inch tube pan. Cut through batter with knife or spatula to remove large air bubbles.

3. Bake at 375°F for 30 to 40 minutes or until top crust is golden brown, firm and dry. Do not underbake. To cool, hang pan upside down on funnel or bottle at least 1½ hours.

4. Remove cake from pan. Trim all crusts from cake. Cut cake into 1-inch cubes. Place half of the cubes in 13×9×2-inch baking dish. Spread with pie filling. Top with layer of remaining cubes.

5. Combine cream cheese and milk; beat until smooth. Fold whipped topping into cream cheese mixture. Spread over cake layer. Refrigerate thoroughly before serving.

CHERRY CRUNCH

12 servings

1   **can (21 ounces) cherry pie filling**
1   **teaspoon lemon juice**
1   **package Duncan Hines Deluxe White Cake Mix**
½   **cup chopped nuts, if desired**
½   **cup (1 stick) butter or margarine, melted Sweetened whipped cream or ice cream**

1. Preheat oven to 350°F.

2. Spread pie filling in bottom of ungreased 8×8×2-inch pan. Sprinkle with lemon juice. Combine dry cake mix, nuts and melted butter (mixture will be crumbly). Sprinkle over pie filling.

3. Bake at 350°F for 40 to 50 minutes or until golden brown. Serve warm with sweetened whipped cream or ice cream.

Cherry Crunch

Apple Custard Dessert

APPLE CUSTARD DESSERT

12 to 16 servings

1 package Duncan Hines
  Butter Recipe Golden
  Cake Mix
1 cup shredded or flaked
  coconut
½ cup (1 stick) butter or
  margarine
6 medium apples, pared,
  cored and cut in eighths
  (about 6 cups)
1 cup water
¼ cup lemon juice

1. Preheat oven to 350°F. Grease 13×9×2-inch baking pan.

2. Combine dry cake mix and coconut in large bowl. Cut in butter with pastry blender or two knives until crumbly.

3. Arrange apple slices in greased pan. Sprinkle crumb mixture over apples. Combine water and lemon juice; pour over all.

4. Bake at 350°F for 45 to 50 minutes or until top is lightly browned and set. Cool before serving.

CHOCOLATE CHEESECAKE

16 servings

1 package Duncan Hines
  Deluxe Deep Chocolate
  Cake Mix
4 large eggs
1 tablespoon Crisco Oil or
  Puritan Oil
2 packages (8 ounces each)
  cream cheese, softened
¾ cup sugar
¼ cup unsweetened cocoa
1½ cups milk
1 teaspoon vanilla extract
2 cups frozen non-dairy
  whipped topping, thawed
  Shaved chocolate,
  if desired

1. Preheat oven to 300°F. Grease 13×9×2-inch pan (see Note). Reserve 1 cup dry cake mix for filling.

2. For crust, mix together remaining dry cake mix, 1 egg and oil (mixture will be crumbly). Press mixture on bottom and three-fourths way up sides of pan.

3. For filling, blend cream cheese, sugar and cocoa in large mixer bowl. Add remaining 3 eggs and reserved 1 cup cake mix. Beat 1 minute at medium speed. Turn to low speed. Add milk and vanilla extract, mixing until smooth. Turn filling into crust.

4. Bake at 300°F for 55 to 65 minutes or until center is firm. Cool to room temperature. Spread whipped topping over cheesecake. Sprinkle with shaved chocolate, if desired. Refrigerate at least 1 hour before serving.

Note: Cheesecake can also be baked in two 9×1½-inch round layer pans for 40 to 50 minutes or until center is firm.

FONDUE PARTY

8 to 12 servings

1 package Duncan Hines
  Deluxe Cake Mix (any
  flavor)
3 large eggs
  Crisco Oil or Puritan Oil
  Water
1 package (14 ounces)
  vanilla caramels
2 ounces (2 squares)
  semisweet chocolate
⅔ cup milk
1 tablespoon corn syrup
  Marshmallows
  Strawberries
  Red maraschino cherries

1. One day before serving, preheat oven to 350°F. Grease and flour 13×9×2-inch pan.

2. Combine dry cake mix, eggs and the amount of oil and water listed on package in large mixer bowl. Mix, bake and cool cake as directed on package. Cut cake into cubes shortly before serving.

3. For fondue, combine caramels, chocolate, milk and corn syrup in heavy saucepan. Cook over low heat, stirring constantly, until caramels and chocolate melt. Pour into fondue pot; keep warm. Add more milk if fondue becomes too thick.

4. Arrange cake cubes, marshmallows, strawberries and cherries on serving tray for dipping.

CHERRY FRUIT 'N' CREAM SQUARES

16 to 20 servings

1 package Duncan Hines
  Deluxe Yellow Cake Mix
½ teaspoon salt
¼ teaspoon baking soda
¾ cup plus 2 tablespoons
  Crisco Oil or Puritan Oil
1 package (8 ounces) cream
  cheese, softened
1 cup confectioners' sugar
1 cup whipped topping
1 can (21 ounces) cherry pie
  filling
  Whipped topping, if
  desired

1. Preheat oven to 350°F.

2. For crust, combine dry cake mix, salt, baking soda and oil. Spread in ungreased 13×9×2-inch pan.

3. Bake at 350°F for 20 minutes or until light brown. Cool.

4. For cream layer, combine cream cheese, confectioners' sugar and whipped topping; mix well. Spread over cooled crust. Carefully spread cherry pie filling over cream layer. Refrigerate at least 1 hour before serving. Decorate with whipped topping, if desired. Store in refrigerator.

BANANA CREAM CHEESECAKE

16 servings

1 package Duncan Hines
  Deluxe Banana Cake Mix
4 large eggs
3 tablespoons Crisco Oil or
  Puritan Oil
⅓ cup plus ½ cup packed
  brown sugar
1 medium banana, peeled
  and sliced
2 packages (8 ounces each)
  cream cheese, softened
1½ cups milk
2 tablespoons lemon juice
2 cups whipped topping

1. Preheat oven to 300°F. Grease 13×9×2-inch pan (see Note). Reserve 1 cup dry cake mix for filling.

2. For crust, mix together remaining cake mix, 1 egg, oil and ⅓ cup brown sugar (mixture will be crumbly). Press mixture evenly on bottom and three-fourths of way up sides of pan. Arrange banana slices on crust.

3. For filling, blend cream cheese with remaining ½ cup brown sugar in large mixer bowl. Add remaining 3 eggs and 1 cup reserved cake mix. Beat 1 minute at medium speed. Turn to low speed. Add milk and lemon juice, mixing until smooth. Turn into crust.

4. Bake at 300°F for 45 to 55 minutes or until center is firm. Cool on rack. Spread topping over cooled cake. Refrigerate until serving time.

Note: Cheesecake can also be baked in two 9×1½-inch round layer pans for 40 to 50 minutes.

CHOCOLATE SWIRL CHEESECAKE

12 to 16 servings

1 package Duncan Hines Deluxe Devil's Food Cake Mix
½ cup Crisco Oil or Puritan Oil
2 envelopes unflavored gelatin
½ cup cold water
⅓ cup all-purpose flour
¾ cup sugar
½ cup milk
4 large eggs, separated
1 package (6 ounces) semisweet chocolate pieces (1 cup)
⅓ cup whipping cream
2 cups creamed cottage cheese
1 teaspoon vanilla extract
½ teaspoon almond extract
1⅓ cups whipped topping

1. Preheat oven to 350°F. Grease 9- or 10-inch springform pan.

2. For crust, combine dry cake mix and oil in bowl; mix well. Turn mixture into pan; press firmly and evenly over bottom.

3. Bake at 350°F for 20 to 25 minutes. Cool on rack.

4. Sprinkle gelatin over cold water to soften. Blend flour and ¼ cup sugar in saucepan. Stir in milk. Cook and stir over medium heat until mixture boils and thickens. Remove from heat. Beat egg yolks with fork; stir a small amount of hot mixture into yolks. Return yolk mixture to saucepan.

5. Cook 1 minute, stirring constantly. Remove from heat. Add softened gelatin; stir until dissolved. Cool to lukewarm.

6. Combine chocolate pieces and whipping cream in heavy saucepan. Heat, stirring constantly, over low heat until chocolate is melted. Cool to lukewarm. Beat cottage cheese 5 minutes at high speed in mixer bowl. Beat in vanilla extract, almond extract and gelatin mixture.

7. Beat egg whites until frothy in mixer bowl. Continue beating, gradually adding ½ cup sugar until stiff peaks form. Fold beaten egg whites into gelatin mixture. Then fold in whipped topping. Spoon one-third filling onto crust, drizzle with chocolate mixture and swirl with spoon, making marble pattern. Repeat with remaining filling and chocolate two more times. Refrigerate 6 hours before serving.

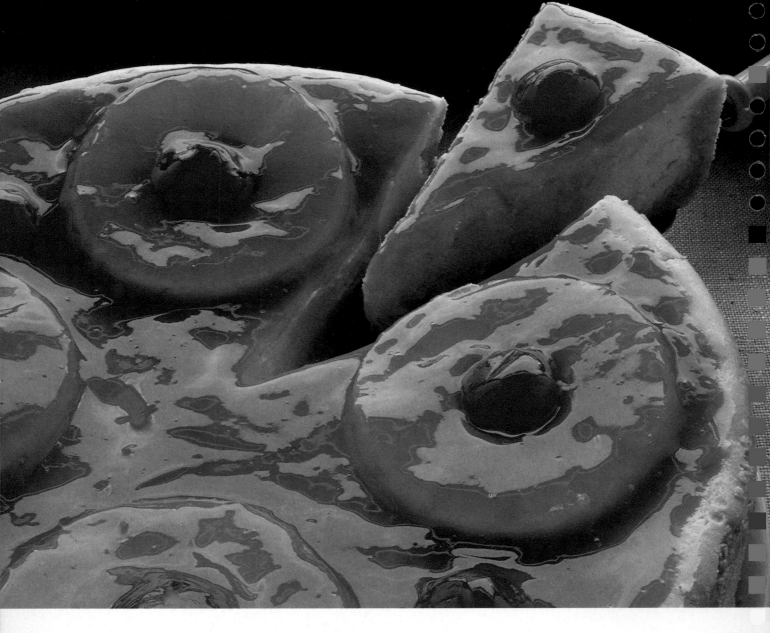

HAWAIIAN CHEESECAKE

12 to 16 servings

1   package Duncan Hines
    Deluxe Pineapple
    Cake Mix
4   *large eggs*
1   *tablespoon Crisco Oil or*
    Puritan Oil
2   *packages (8 ounces each)*
    cream cheese, softened
½   *cup sugar*
1½ *cups milk*
1   *tablespoon vanilla extract*
1   *can (8 ounces) sliced*
    pineapple in juice
2   *teaspoons cornstarch*
2   *tablespoons red*
    maraschino cherry syrup
6   *red maraschino cherries*

1. Preheat oven to 300°F. Grease 10-inch springform pan. Reserve 1 cup dry cake mix.

2. For crust, combine remaining dry cake mix, 1 egg and oil in large bowl until crumbly. Press crumb mixture on bottom and halfway up sides of pan.

3. For filling, blend cream cheese and sugar in large mixer bowl. Add remaining 3 eggs and 1 cup reserved cake mix. Beat 1 minute at medium speed. Gradually add milk and vanilla extract, blending at low speed until smooth. Pour filling into crumb-lined pan.

4. Bake at 300°F for 60 to 70 minutes or until center is firm. Cool in pan on rack. Remove sides of pan.

5. Drain pineapple, reserving juice. Blend reserved pineapple juice and cornstarch in small saucepan. Cook and stir over medium heat until mixture boils and thickens, about 3 minutes. Stir in cherry syrup; cool slightly. Arrange pineapple slices and maraschino cherries on top of cooled cheesecake. Spoon slightly cooled glaze over fruits and cheesecake. Refrigerate until ready to serve.

YOGURT DESSERT SQUARES

16 servings

1 *package Duncan Hines Deluxe White Cake Mix*
4 *large eggs*
2 *cartons (8 ounces each) vanilla or other flavored yogurt*
1 *cup milk*
2 *tablespoons lemon juice Topping: yogurt, pie filling, whipped cream or fresh fruit*

1. Preheat oven to 300°F. Grease 13×9×2-inch pan. Reserve 1½ cups dry cake mix.

2. For crust, mix together remaining cake mix and 1 egg in large bowl (mixture will be crumbly). Press crumb mixture evenly on bottom of pan.

3. For filling, combine reserved cake mix, 2 cartons yogurt and 3 eggs in large mixer bowl. Beat 1 minute at medium speed. Turn to low speed. Add milk and lemon juice, mixing until smooth. Pour into crust.

4. Bake at 300°F for 55 to 60 minutes or until center is firm. Cool on rack. Top with your favorite topping. Refrigerate until serving time. To serve, cut into squares.

APRICOT CRUNCH

8 to 10 servings

2 *cans (16 ounces each) apricot halves, drained*
1 *cup plus 3 tablespoons packed brown sugar*
1 *package Duncan Hines Deluxe White Cake Mix*
½ *cup (1 stick) butter or margarine, melted*
½ *cup chopped nuts, if desired Dairy sour cream, sweetened whipped cream or ice cream*

1. Preheat oven to 350°F.

2. Arrange apricots in ungreased 9×9×2-inch pan. Sprinkle with 3 tablespoons brown sugar. Combine dry cake mix, melted butter, remaining 1 cup brown sugar and nuts, if desired. (Mixture will be crumbly). Sprinkle over apricots.

3. Bake at 350°F for 40 to 50 minutes or until golden brown. Serve warm topped with sour cream, whipped cream or ice cream.

BAKED CHOCOLATE ALASKA

12 to 16 servings

1 *package Duncan Hines Deluxe Devil's Food Cake Mix*
3 *large eggs*
½ *cup Crisco Oil or Puritan Oil*
1⅓ *cups water*
1 *quart butter pecan or coffee ice cream, softened*
4 *egg whites*
⅛ *teaspoon cream of tartar*
½ *cup sugar*
1 *teaspoon vanilla extract*

1. Preheat oven to 350°F. Grease and flour two 9×9×2-inch pans or two 9×1½-inch round layer pans.

2. Combine dry cake mix, whole eggs, oil and water in large mixer bowl. Mix cake as directed on package. Divide batter evenly into pans.

3. Bake at 350°F for 30 to 35 minutes or until toothpick inserted in centers comes out clean. Cool in pans on racks 10 minutes. Remove from pans; cool completely on racks.

4. Line 9-inch square or round pan with waxed paper. Spoon softened ice cream into pan and spread evenly. Wrap tightly and freeze until firm.

5. Place one cooled cake layer on heatproof plate or cookie sheet. Unmold ice cream layer onto cake layer and peel off paper. Place remaining layer on ice cream layer. Set in freezer. When ready to serve, preheat oven to 450°F.

6. For meringue, beat egg whites and cream of tartar in bowl until frothy. Add sugar, 1 tablespoon at a time, beating well after each addition. Continue beating until meringue is stiff and glossy. Beat in vanilla extract. Spread meringue over top and sides of cake to cover completely.

7. Bake at 450°F for 4 to 6 minutes or until merigue is golden brown. Serve immediately or return to freezer until ready to serve.

Muffins, Loaves & Coffee Cakes

GOLDEN FRUIT LOAVES

2 medium loaves

1 package Duncan Hines Butter Recipe Golden Cake Mix
1½ cups chopped candied mixed fruit (6 ounces)
½ cup all-purpose flour
½ teaspoon baking powder
½ teaspoon baking soda
1 cup milk
2 large eggs
2 tablespoons butter or margarine, softened

1. Preheat oven to 350°F. Grease and flour two 8½×4½×2½-inch loaf pans.

2. Sprinkle 2 tablespoons dry cake mix over dried fruit; stir to coat.

3. Combine remaining cake mix, flour, baking powder and baking soda in large mixer bowl. Add milk, eggs and butter. Blend at low speed, then beat 2 minutes at medium speed. Fold in fruit. Divide batter evenly in pans.

4. Bake at 350°F for 45 to 50 minutes or until toothpick inserted in center comes out clean. Cool in pans on racks 20 minutes. Remove from pans; cool completely on racks.

CARROT MUFFINS

24 muffins

1 package Duncan Hines Deluxe Carrot Cake Mix
2 tablespoons all-purpose flour
1 teaspoon baking powder
¼ cup chopped nuts
⅔ cup milk
3 large eggs
⅓ cup Crisco Oil or Puritan Oil
6 tablespoons sugar
1 teaspoon ground cinnamon
¼ cup (½ stick) butter or margarine, melted

1. Preheat oven to 375°F. Grease 24 muffin cups or line with paper baking cups.

2. Combine dry cake mix, flour, baking powder and nuts in large bowl. Beat milk, eggs and oil together with fork in another bowl; add to dry mixture, stirring just until dry ingredients are moistened. Spoon batter into muffin cups, filling about one-third full.

3. Bake at 375°F for 15 to 20 minutes or until golden brown. Cool 5 minutes; remove from pans.

4. For topping, combine sugar and cinnamon. Dip muffin tops in melted butter and then in cinnamon-sugar.

BANANA MUFFINS

24 muffins

1 package Duncan Hines Deluxe Banana Cake Mix
2 tablespoons all-purpose flour
1 teaspoon baking powder
¼ cup chopped nuts
¾ cup plus 2 tablespoons milk
2 large eggs

1. Preheat oven to 375°F. Grease 24 muffin cups or line with paper baking cups.

2. Combine dry cake mix, flour, baking powder and nuts in large bowl. Beat milk and eggs together with fork; add to mixture in bowl and stir just until dry ingredients are moistened.

3. Spoon batter into muffin cups, filling one-third full.

4. Bake at 375°F for 15 to 20 minutes or until golden brown.

Golden Fruit Loaves (top),
Carrot Muffins (bottom)

APPLE BRUNCH CAKE

12 to 16 servings

1 package Duncan Hines
  Butter Recipe Golden
  Cake Mix
3 large eggs
½ cup (1 stick) butter or
  margarine, softened
⅔ cup water
4 apples, pared, cored and
  sliced (about 4 cups)
3 tablespoons sugar
4 teaspoons ground
  cinnamon
  Confectioners' sugar

1. Preheat oven to 375°F. Grease and flour 10-inch tube pan.

2. Combine dry cake mix, eggs, butter and water in large mixer bowl. Mix cake as directed on package. Turn two-thirds batter into pan. Toss apples with sugar and cinnamon. Spoon over batter in pan. Spread remaining batter over apples.

3. Bake at 375°F for 45 to 50 minutes or until toothpick inserted in center comes out clean. Cool in pan on rack 25 minutes. Remove from pan; cool completely on rack. Sprinkle cooled cake with confectioners' sugar.

PLUM KUCHEN

12 to 16 servings

1 package Duncan Hines
  Deluxe White Cake Mix
¾ cup (1½ sticks) butter or
  margarine, divided
2 large eggs, beaten
⅓ cup milk
1 teaspoon vanilla extract
6 fresh plums, pitted and cut
  into eighths
1 cup seedless white grapes
¼ cup sugar
1 teaspoon ground
  cinnamon
  Sweetened whipped
  cream, if desired

1. Preheat oven to 400°F. Lightly grease 13×9×2-inch pan.

2. Place dry cake mix in large bowl. Cut in ½ cup butter with pastry blender or 2 knives until mixture resembles coarse crumbs. Add eggs, milk and vanilla extract; stir with fork until smooth. Turn batter into pan and spread evenly. Arrange plum pieces in parallel rows over batter; arrange grapes between rows.

3. For topping, melt ¼ cup butter. Stir in sugar and cinnamon. Spoon over fruit.

4. Bake at 400°F for 33 to 37 minutes or until fruit is tender. Cool in pan on rack 30 minutes. Serve warm, topped with sweetened whipped cream, if desired.

BREAKFAST SPECIAL

16 to 20 servings

½ cup all-purpose flour
¼ cup granulated sugar
2 tablespoons butter or
  margarine, softened
1 package Duncan Hines
  Deluxe Yellow Cake Mix
1 cup water
3 large eggs
½ cup (1 stick) butter or
  margarine, softened
1½ teaspoons vanilla extract
½ cup confectioners' sugar
1 tablespoon water

1. Preheat oven to 350°F. Grease and flour two 9×1½-inch round layer pans.

2. For topping, combine flour and granulated sugar in small bowl. Stir in 2 tablespoons butter until mixture is crumbly; set aside.

3. Combine dry cake mix, 1 cup water, eggs, ½ cup butter and vanilla extract in large mixer bowl. Mix as directed on package. Pour batter evenly into pans. Sprinkle topping evenly over each cake.

4. Bake at 350°F for 30 to 35 minutes or until toothpick inserted in center comes out clean. Cool in pans on racks.

5. For glaze*, combine confectioners' sugar and 1 tablespoon water; blend well. Drizzle over cooled cakes.

Or, heat ⅔ cup Duncan Hines Vanilla Frosting in small saucepan over medium heat, stirring constantly, until thin.

ORANGE WAKE-UP CAKE

12 to 16 servings

1 package Duncan Hines
  Butter Recipe Golden
  Cake Mix
⅔ cup water
3 large eggs
½ cup (1 stick) butter or
  margarine, softened
2 tablespoons grated orange
  peel
½ cup chopped pecans
⅓ cup packed brown sugar
¼ cup fine graham cracker
  crumbs
2 tablespoons butter or
  margarine, melted
1½ teaspoons ground
  cinnamon
1 cup confectioners' sugar
2 tablespoons hot water
¼ teaspoon vanilla extract

1. Preheat oven to 375°F. Grease and flour two 9×1½-inch round layer pans.

2. Combine dry cake mix, water, eggs and ½ cup butter in large mixer bowl. Mix cake as directed on package. Fold in 1 tablespoon of the orange peel. Divide batter evenly in pans.

3. For topping, combine pecans, brown sugar, graham cracker crumbs, 2 tablespoons butter, remaining orange peel and cinnamon; mix well. Sprinkle evenly over batter in pans.

4. Bake at 375°F for 25 to 30 minutes or until toothpick inserted in center comes out clean.

5. For glaze*, mix confectioners' sugar, hot water and vanilla until smooth. Drizzle over warm cakes. Serve warm or cool in pans.

*Or heat ⅔ cup Duncan Hines Vanilla Frosting in a small saucepan over medium heat, stirring constantly, until thin.

GOLDEN OATMEAL MUFFINS

24 muffins

1 package Duncan Hines
  Butter Recipe Golden
  Cake Mix
1 cup quick-cooking oats
¼ teaspoon salt
¾ cup milk
2 large eggs, slightly beaten
2 tablespoons butter or
  margarine, melted
  Honey or jam

1. Preheat oven to 400°F. Grease 24 muffin cups.

2. Combine dry cake mix, oats and salt in bowl. Beat together milk, eggs and butter. Add to dry ingredients, stirring just until moistened. Spoon into muffin cups, filling two-thirds full.

3. Bake at 400°F for 13 minutes or until golden brown. Serve with honey or your favorite jam.

GALA CHERRY BREAD

2 medium loaves

1 package Duncan Hines
  Deluxe Cherry Cake Mix
1 cup all-purpose flour
1¼ cups water
3 large eggs
⅓ cup Crisco Oil or
  Puritan Oil
1 cup chopped pecans
½ cup semisweet chocolate
  pieces
¼ cup coarsely chopped red
  maraschino cherries, well
  drained

1. Preheat oven to 350°F. Grease two 8½×4½×2½-inch loaf pans. Line bottoms with waxed paper; grease.

2. Combine dry cake mix and flour in large mixer bowl. Add water, eggs and oil; mix to blend, then beat 2 minutes at medium speed. Stir in pecans, chocolate pieces and cherries. Divide batter evenly into pans.

3. Bake at 350°F for 53 to 58 minutes or until toothpick inserted in center comes out clean. Cool in pans 15 minutes; remove from pans and peel off paper. Cool completely on racks.

BANANA STREUSEL CAKE

12 to 16 servings

½ cup all-purpose flour
¼ cup packed brown sugar
2 teaspoons ground
  cinnamon
2 tablespoons butter or
  margarine, softened
1 package Duncan Hines
  Deluxe Banana Cake Mix
3 large eggs
½ cup (1 stick) butter or
  margarine, softened
1 cup water
1½ teaspoons vanilla extract
1 cup confectioners' sugar
1 tablespoon water

1. Preheat oven to 375°F. Grease and flour 10-inch tube pan.

2. For streusel, combine flour, brown sugar and cinnamon in small bowl. Mix in 2 tablespoons butter until mixture is crumbly.

3. For cake, combine dry cake mix, eggs, ½ cup butter, 1 cup water and vanilla extract in large mixer bowl. Mix as directed on package. Spoon one-third of batter into pan; sprinkle with streusel. Repeat two more times, ending with streusel.

4. Bake at 375°F for 42 to 48 minutes or until toothpick inserted in center comes out clean. Cool in pan on rack for 25 minutes; remove from pan.

5. For glaze,* combine confectioners' sugar and 1 tablespoon water in small bowl; mix until smooth. Drizzle over warm cake.

Or heat ⅔ cup Duncan Hines Vanilla Frosting in small saucepan over medium heat, stirring constantly, until thin.

Golden Oatmeal Muffins

BANANA NUT BREAD

2 medium loaves

4 ounces cream cheese,
  softened
2 large eggs
3 medium bananas, peeled
  and mashed
1 package Duncan Hines
  Deluxe Yellow Cake Mix
¾ cup chopped nuts

1. Preheat oven to 350°F. Grease two 8½×4½×2½-inch loaf pans.

2. Put cream cheese and eggs in small mixer bowl; blend at low speed until smooth. Add mashed bananas; mix well. Place half of dry cake mix in large bowl. Add banana mixture and beat until blended. Add remaining cake mix and nuts; stir just until blended. Divide batter evenly in pans.

3. Bake at 350°F for 35 to 45 minutes or until toothpick inserted in center comes out clean. Cool in pans on racks 20 minutes. Remove from pans; cool completely on racks.

EASY APPLE KUCHEN

24 servings

2 envelopes active dry yeast
¼ cup warm water (about
  110°F)
2 large eggs
1 package Duncan Hines
  Deluxe Yellow Cake Mix
1¼ cups all-purpose flour
1½ cups sugar
1 tablespoon ground
  cinnamon
⅓ cup butter or margarine
6 medium apples or 2 cans
  (20 ounces each)
  pie-sliced apples, drained

1. Dissolve yeast in warm water in large mixer bowl. Blend in eggs and half of dry cake mix. Beat for 1 minute at medium speed. Add remaining cake mix and beat for 3 minutes at medium speed. (Batter should be quite stiff but not doughlike.) Let rest 5 minutes.

2. Sprinkle flour on board. Scrape batter out onto prepared board. Knead batter until flour is worked in, about 100 strokes. Place in greased bowl, cover, and let rise in warm, draft-free place for 30 minutes.

3. For topping, mix sugar and cinnamon in bowl; cut in butter with pastry blender or 2 knives.

4. Preheat oven to 350°F. Grease 13×9×2-inch pan and 8×8×2-inch pan. Pare, core and slice apples.

5. Punch down dough with greased fingertips. Spread dough to ¼- to ⅓-inch thickness on bottom of pans. Arrange apple slices in rows on top. Sprinkle with topping. Let rise in warm place for 30 minutes.

6. Bake at 350°F for 25 to 30 minutes or until toothpick inserted in center comes out clean. Serve warm.

Easy Apple Kuchen

Carrot Apple Streusel Cake

CARROT APPLE STREUSEL CAKE

16 servings

1 package Duncan Hines Deluxe Carrot Cake Mix
1¾ teaspoons ground cinnamon
3 large eggs, slightly beaten
½ cup applesauce
⅓ cup Crisco Oil or Puritan Oil
3 baking apples, pared, cored, and cut into eighths
½ cup all-purpose flour
2 tablespoons sugar
¼ cup (½ stick) butter or margarine

1. Preheat oven to 350°F. Grease and flour two 9×1½-inch round layer pans.

2. Combine dry cake mix and ½ teaspoon cinnamon in large bowl. Combine eggs, applesauce and oil; add to dry ingredients and mix thoroughly with wooden spoon. Divide batter evenly in pans. Arrange sliced apples on top.

3. For streusel, combine flour, sugar and 1¼ teaspoons cinnamon in small bowl. Cut in butter with pastry blender or 2 knives until crumbly. Sprinkle evenly over apples.

4. Bake at 350°F for 28 to 33 minutes or until toothpick inserted in center comes out clean. Cool in pan 10 minutes. Serve warm.

SOUR CREAM BRUNCH CAKE

12 to 16 servings

1 package Duncan Hines Deluxe Yellow Cake Mix
1 cup dairy sour cream
4 large eggs
½ cup Crisco Oil or Puritan Oil
1 package (4-serving-size) vanilla instant pudding and pie filling mix
2 teaspoons vanilla extract
⅓ cup sugar
1 teaspoon unsweetened cocoa
1 teaspoon ground cinnamon
½ cup chopped nuts

1. Preheat oven to 350°F. Grease and flour 10-inch tube pan.

2. Combine dry cake mix, sour cream, eggs, oil, pudding mix and vanilla extract in large mixer bowl. Beat 4 minutes at medium speed. Turn half of batter into pan.

3. Combine sugar, cocoa, cinnamon and nuts. Sprinkle half of cocoa mixture over batter in pan. Add remaining batter and sprinkle with remaining topping.

4. Bake at 350°F for 50 to 55 minutes or until toothpick inserted in center comes out clean. Cool cake completely on rack before removing from pan.

APPLE OATMEAL LOAF

1 large loaf

1 package Duncan Hines
  Deluxe Apple Cake Mix
½ cup plus 2 tablespoons
  quick-cooking oats
3 large eggs
⅓ cup Crisco Oil or Puritan
  Oil
1¼ cups water

1. Preheat oven to 350°F. Grease and flour 9×5×3-inch loaf pan.

2. Combine dry cake mix, ½ cup oats, eggs, oil and water in large mixer bowl. Mix cake as directed on package. Turn batter into pan. Sprinkle with remaining 2 tablespoons oats.

3. Bake at 350°F for 55 to 65 minutes or until toothpick inserted in center comes out clean. Cool in pan on rack 15 to 20 minutes. Remove from pan; cool completely on rack.

APRICOT STREUSEL COFFEE CAKE

16 servings

1 package Duncan Hines
  Deluxe Yellow Cake Mix
3 large eggs
⅓ cup Crisco Oil or Puritan
  Oil
1 cup water
2 cans (16 ounces each)
  apricot halves, drained
2 teaspoons ground
  cinnamon
1 teaspoon ground nutmeg
3 tablespoons brown sugar

1. Preheat oven to 350°F. Grease and flour 13×9×2-inch pan. Measure 2 tablespoons dry cake mix and set aside.

2. Combine remaining dry cake mix, eggs, oil and water in large mixer bowl. Mix cake as directed on package. Turn batter into pan and spread evenly.

3. Arrange drained apricot halves in rows on top of batter. Combine 2 tablespoons reserved cake mix, cinnamon, nutmeg and brown sugar. Sprinkle mixture over apricots.

4. Bake at 350°F for 40 to 45 minutes or until toothpick inserted in center comes out clean. Allow cake to cool 1 hour on rack before serving.

BLUEBERRY MUFFINS

24 muffins

1 package Duncan Hines
  Deluxe White Cake Mix
2 tablespoons all-purpose
  flour
1 teaspoon baking powder
⅔ cup milk
3 large eggs
⅓ cup Crisco Oil or Puritan
  Oil
1 cup rinsed fresh or
  well-drained, thawed,
  frozen blueberries

1. Preheat oven to 375°F. Line 24 muffin cups with paper liners.

2. Combine dry cake mix, flour and baking powder in large bowl. Beat milk, eggs and oil together with fork; add to mixture in bowl and stir just until dry ingredients are moistened. Fold in blueberries.

3. Spoon batter into muffin cups, filling one-third full.

4. Bake at 375°F for 15 to 20 minutes or until golden brown.

FUDGE MARBLE STREUSEL CAKE

12 to 16 servings

1 package Duncan Hines
  Deluxe Fudge Marble
  Cake Mix
½ cup sugar
¼ cup all-purpose flour
¼ cup flaked coconut
2 tablespoons butter or
  margarine, melted
1⅓ cups water
3 large eggs
⅓ cup Crisco Oil or
  Puritan Oil

1. Preheat oven to 375°F. Grease and flour 10-inch tube pan.

2. For streusel, combine contents of cake mix small packet, sugar, flour, coconut and melted butter; set aside.

3. Combine dry cake mix, water, eggs and oil in large mixer bowl. Mix cake as directed on package. Turn three-quarters of batter into pan and spread evenly. Measure ⅓ cup streusel and set aside. Sprinkle remaining streusel over batter. Spread with remaining batter and sprinkle with remaining streusel.

4. Bake at 375°F for 40 to 50 minutes or until toothpick inserted in center comes out clean. Cool in pan on rack 25 minutes, then remove from pan. Serve warm.

Apple Oatmeal Loaf

CINNAMON STREUSEL CAKE

12 to 16 servings

½ cup all-purpose flour
¼ cup packed brown sugar
2 teaspoons ground cinnamon
2 tablespoon butter or margarine, softened
1 package Duncan Hines Deluxe Yellow Cake Mix
3 large eggs
½ cup (1 stick) butter or margarine, softened
1 cup water
1½ teaspoons vanilla extract
1 cup confectioners' sugar
2 tablespoons water

1. Preheat oven to 375°F. Grease and flour 10-inch tube pan.

2. For streusel, combine flour, brown sugar, cinnamon and 2 tablespoons butter in small bowl. Mix until mixture is crumbly.

3. Combine dry cake mix, eggs, ½ cup butter, 1 cup water and vanilla extract in large mixer bowl. Mix cake as directed on package. Spoon one-third of batter into pan; sprinkle with one-third of streusel. Repeat two more times, ending with streusel.

4. Bake at 375°F for 42 to 48 minutes or until toothpick inserted in center comes out clean. Cool in pan 20 minutes; remove from pan.

5. For glaze,* combine confectioners' sugar and 2 tablespoons water in small bowl. Mix until smooth. Drizzle over warm cake.

Or heat ⅔ cup Duncan Hines Vanilla Frosting in small saucepan over medium heat, stirring constantly, until thin.

APPLE RAISIN MUFFINS

24 muffins

1 package Duncan Hines Deluxe Apple Cake Mix
2 tablespoons all-purpose flour
1 teaspoon baking powder
⅔ cup milk
3 large eggs
⅓ cup Crisco Oil or Puritan Oil
½ cup chopped apple
½ cup chopped raisins

1. Preheat oven to 375°F. Line 24 muffin cups with paper baking cups.

2. Combine dry cake mix, flour and baking powder in large bowl. Beat milk, eggs and oil together with fork; add to mixture in bowl and stir until dry ingredients are moistened. Fold in chopped apple and raisins. Spoon batter into muffin cups, filling about two-thirds full.

3. Bake at 375°F for 15 to 20 minutes or until golden brown.

NEAPOLITAN STREUSEL COFFEE CAKE

16 servings

1 package Duncan Hines Deluxe Fudge Marble Cake Mix
1 envelope active dry yeast
1 cup all-purpose flour
2 large eggs
⅔ cup warm water
1 can (21 ounces) strawberry pie filling
5 tablespoons butter or margarine, melted
½ cup chopped nuts
1 cup confectioners' sugar
2 tablespoons water

1. Preheat oven to 350°F. Grease 13×9×2-inch pan. Reserve cake mix small packet.

2. Combine 1½ cups dry cake mix, yeast, flour, eggs and ⅔ cup warm water in large mixer bowl. Blend, then beat 2 minutes at medium speed.

3. Spread dough in pan. Spoon strawberry pie filling evenly over dough.

4. For streusel, combine reserved cake mix, contents of small packet, melted butter and nuts; sprinkle over strawberry filling.

5. Bake at 350°F for 30 minutes.

6. For glaze*, mix confectioners' sugar and 2 tablespoons water until smooth. Drizzle over coffee cake.

Or heat ⅔ cup Duncan Hines Vanilla Frosting in small saucepan over medium heat, stirring constantly, until thin.

Index